Wild! Wonderful!

A Cookbook With Flair

PRESENTED BY THE JUNIOR LEAGUE OF WHEELING

Wild! Wonderful!

A Cookbook With Flair

Library of Congress Control Number: 2003102747

ISBN: 0-9613428-2-X

Edited, Designed, and Manufactured by

Favorite Recipes® Press

An imprint of

FRP

PO Box 305142

Nashville, Tennessee 37230, 1-800-358-0560

Manufactured in the United States of America

First Printing 2003   10,000 copies

Cover Art: *"Pennsylvania Railroad Wall"* by Janet Rodriguez. Mrs. Rodriguez resides in Wheeling and actively instructs in the art of watercolor painting. Her initial art education was in oil and pastels, but after discovering watercolors, she states, *"I've never wanted to do anything else, and I've never looked back."*

Cookbook Committee

Karen Blair, Co-Chairperson
Debbie Wilkinson, Co-Chairperson

Marketing
Cristen Breski
Christine Kuhn

Non-Recipe Text/Art Design
Saun Capehart
Rhonda Hager

Recipes
Sarah Barickman
Alecia Blair
Dawn Nazzaro

Honorary Members
Ginny Favede
Shawn Turak

Special thanks to the entire membership for their recipes,
testing, and assistance in many ways.

A very special thank you to our husbands, who endured
all this project had to "dish" out.

Mission Statement

The Association of Junior Leagues International, Inc., is an organization of women committed to promoting voluntarism, developing the potential of women, and improving communities through the effective action and leadership of trained volunteers. Its purpose is exclusively educational and charitable.

Position Statements

Voluntarism—The Junior League of Wheeling, Inc., supports and promotes voluntarism as an essential component of our society and will take action to ensure the continued effectiveness of the voluntary sector.

Youth—The Junior League of Wheeling, Inc., is committed to ensuring that the children have the opportunities and services essential for physical, intellectual, emotional, mental, and social growth, as well as their personal safety, and will advocate that such opportunities and services are provided.

Revitalization—The Junior League of Wheeling, Inc., recognizes the need to support these programs, which promote economic development, historic restoration and preservation, and tourism, and will advocate to promote such programs that will enhance the revitalization of the Upper Ohio Valley.

Arts—The Junior League of Wheeling, Inc., supports growth and enrichment in all areas of Arts and Humanities and is committed to providing the opportunities for their appreciation by the community.

Wellness—The Junior League of Wheeling, Inc., supports the ideal of a productive, healthy and emotionally enriched life, and supports those programs and legislation which further these concepts.

Table of Contents

CHAPTER ONE

CHAPTER TWO

CHAPTER THREE

CHAPTER FOUR

CHAPTER FIVE

CHAPTER SIX

CHAPTER SEVEN

CHAPTER EIGHT

CHAPTER NINE

CHAPTER TEN

Introduction

Wheeling, "The Friendly City" or "The City of Lights," is more than just a wonderful place to live and raise a family. As you will see in paging through this marvelous cookbook, Wheeling and the Ohio Valley is a fabulous place to visit. The Ohio Valley is rich with history, tradition, heritage, and the beauty of The Mountain State.

The Junior League of Wheeling, Inc., is proud to serve to you this cookbook, which celebrates the rich diversity found in the Ohio Valley. Recipes—from Wild to Wonderful—make this a cookbook, and truly a community, with Flair.

The Junior League of Wheeling, Inc., is one of the many longstanding traditions in the community. For more than sixty years since its founding in 1940, The Junior League of Wheeling has enriched the community through its community projects and with many trained volunteers. Notable contributions to the Ohio Valley include spearheading, planning, and building of the Heritage Port Playground, an all-community build project that involved hundreds of volunteers, thousands of dollars, and countless hours of manpower. The Junior League of Wheeling, Inc., an organization exclusive to women, built the State of West Virginia's first "All Women's Build," partnering with Habitat for Humanity.

Most recently, The Junior League of Wheeling, Inc., adopted as its signature project the creation of a Child Advocacy Center, one of the first in the State of West Virginia. The Child Advocacy Center will serve as a house of comfort to children who are victims of abuse, while they undergo a single forensic interview by a trained professional. The single interview, assisted by a multidisciplinary team of law enforcement, social services, and medical specialists, will eliminate inflicting additional trauma on the victim each time he or she is asked to tell his or her story of abuse.

We proudly present to you **Wild! Wonderful! A Cookbook with Flair**. Your purchase of this cookbook enables The Junior League of Wheeling, Inc., to continue its tradition of serving the community. So, bon appétit. Enjoy this treasured cookbook, knowing that by supporting The Junior League of Wheeling, Inc., you support the community in which we live.

Breakfast With Champions

The Ohio Valley is rich in athletic tradition and is home to many "Hall of Famers." From the area's youth sports leagues to the Ohio Valley Athletic Conference for high school teams, the Ohio Valley boasts many talented athletes who develop their athletic prowess on area fields before heading off to college and professional arenas.

Local professional sports teams have a flair both on the field and the ice. The Ohio Valley Greyhound Arena Football Team and the Wheeling Nailers Hockey Team have given fans a true taste of athleticism and success.

A good sporting event begins with dedicated teams like a good day begins with a great breakfast.

An untitled piece by Diana Carney, a high school senior who resides in Moundsville, West Virginia. Diana favors painting with acrylics and plans to pursue a career in art-based advertising. She lists "whatever strikes my interest" as her choice of subjects.

Ham Rolls with Swiss Cheese

1/2 cup (1 stick) margarine, softened
1 medium onion, grated
3 tablespoons prepared mustard
2 tablespoons poppy seeds
1 teaspoon Worcestershire sauce
2 (20-count) packages small party
*   rolls or potato rolls*
3/4 pound ham, finely chopped
1 1/2 cups (6 ounces) shredded
*   Swiss cheese*

Combine the margarine, onion, prepared mustard, poppy seeds and Worcestershire sauce in a bowl and mix well. Split the rolls lengthwise, cutting to but not through the other side. Spread the margarine mixture on the bottom half of each roll. Add ham and cheese to each roll. Cover with the roll tops. Place the rolls on a baking sheet and cover with foil. Bake at 350 degrees for 30 to 40 minutes or until the cheese melts.

Yield: 40 rolls

Note: Substitute sliced ham and cheese if you wish. To prepare the rolls for future use, wrap them tightly in foil and freeze. Bake the rolls right from the freezer, but be sure to allow extra time in the oven.

Mexican Egg Casserole

12 eggs, lightly beaten
1/2 cup flour
1 teaspoon baking powder
1/2 cup (1 stick) butter, melted
2 (4-ounce) cans diced green
*   chiles*
16 ounces cottage cheese
4 cups (16 ounces) shredded
*   Monterey Jack cheese*
1 pound ham, diced (optional)

Combine the eggs, flour and baking powder in a bowl and mix lightly, leaving the mixture lumpy. Add the butter, green chiles, cottage cheese, Monterey Jack cheese and ham and mix well. Pour into a greased 9×13-inch baking dish. Bake at 400 degrees for 15 minutes. Reduce the heat to 350 degrees. Bake for 35 to 40 minutes longer.

Yield: 6 to 10 servings

12

Sausage and Spinach Breakfast Casserole

2¹/2 cups seasoned croutons
1 pound bulk pork sausage
4 eggs
2¹/4 cups milk
1 (10-ounce) can cream of
   mushroom soup
1 (10-ounce) package frozen
   chopped spinach, thawed and
   squeezed dry
1 cup (4 ounces) shredded sharp
   Cheddar cheese
1 cup (4 ounces) shredded
   Monterey Jack cheese
¹/4 teaspoon dry mustard

Spread the croutons in a single layer in a greased 9×13-inch baking dish. Brown the sausage in a skillet over medium heat, stirring until crumbly; drain. Layer the sausage over the croutons. Whisk the eggs and milk in a bowl. Stir in the cream of mushroom soup, spinach, Cheddar cheese, Monterey Jack cheese and dry mustard. Pour the egg mixture over the sausage. Chill, covered, for 8 to 10 hours. Let stand at room temperature for 30 minutes. Remove the cover. Bake at 325 degrees for 50 to 55 minutes or until lightly browned and set. Let stand for a few minutes before serving.

Yield: 10 to 12 servings

Breakfast Casserole

4 slices bread, toasted
1 pound bulk pork sausage, sliced
1¹/₂ cups (6 ounces) shredded
    Cheddar cheese
6 eggs, beaten
2 cups half-and-half
¹/₂ teaspoon salt

Cut the toast into strips. Arrange in a single layer in a buttered 9×9-inch baking dish. Cook the sausage in a skillet until browned; drain. Arrange the sausage over the toast. Sprinkle with the cheese. Pour a mixture of the eggs, half-and-half and salt over the cheese. Chill, covered, for 8 to 10 hours. Let stand at room temperature for 30 minutes. Bake, uncovered, at 350 degrees for 45 minutes or until golden brown. Let stand for a few minutes before serving.

Yield: 6 to 8 servings

Note: Mushrooms, onions and peppers may be added for variety. A little salsa will give the dish a Mexican kick.

13

Egg Casserole

1 to 1¹/₂ pounds hot bulk pork
    sausage
9 eggs, lightly beaten
3 cups milk
1¹/₂ teaspoons dry mustard
1 teaspoon salt
3 slices white bread, crusts
    removed and cubed
1¹/₂ cups (6 ounces) shredded
    sharp Cheddar cheese

Brown the sausage in a skillet, stirring until crumbly; drain. Combine the eggs, milk, dry mustard and salt in a large bowl and mix well. Stir in the sausage, bread and cheese. Pour the mixture into a greased 9×13-inch baking dish. Chill, covered, for 8 to 10 hours. Let stand at room temperature for 30 minutes. Remove the cover. Bake at 350 degrees for 1 hour or until golden brown.

Yield: 10 to 12 servings

14

Summer Quiche

1 unbaked (9-inch) pie shell
1 small red bell pepper, chopped
1/2 small red onion, chopped
2 garlic cloves, minced
2 tablespoons olive oil
1 1/2 tablespoons chopped
    fresh basil
4 eggs
1 cup half-and-half
1 teaspoon salt
1/2 teaspoon pepper
2 cups (8 ounces) shredded
    Monterey Jack cheese
1/3 cup grated Parmesan cheese
3 Roma tomatoes, sliced
    1/4 inch thick

Fit the pie shell into a 9-inch quiche pan. Prick the bottom and sides with a fork. Bake at 425 degrees for 10 minutes. Remove from the oven. Sauté the bell pepper, onion and garlic in the olive oil in a skillet for 5 minutes or until tender. Stir in the basil. Whisk the eggs, half-and-half, salt and pepper in a large bowl. Stir in the vegetable mixture, Monterey Jack cheese and Parmesan cheese. Pour into the piecrust and top with the tomato slices. Bake at 375 degrees for 45 to 50 minutes or until set. Cover the edges of the piecrust with foil after the first 30 minutes to prevent browning. Let stand for 5 to 10 minutes before cutting.

Yield: 6 to 8 servings

Note: You may prepare the quiche the night before. Chill, covered, for 8 to 10 hours. Let stand at room temperature for 30 minutes before baking.

Cheddar Cheese and Artichoke Breakfast Strata

3 tablespoons butter, softened
10 slices white bread
2 cups (8 ounces) shredded sharp
   Cheddar cheese
1/2 cup roasted red bell pepper,
   cubed
1 (14-ounce) can artichoke hearts,
   drained and coarsely chopped
2 cups milk
6 eggs
1 tablespoon Dijon mustard
1/2 teaspoon dry mustard
1/2 teaspoon salt
1/4 teaspoon pepper
2 tablespoons minced onion, or
   1 teaspoon onion powder

Spread the butter thinly over the bread slices. Cut the bread slices into 1/2-inch strips. Layer 1/2 of the bread strips, 1/2 of the cheese, 1/2 of the bell pepper and 1/2 of the artichoke hearts in a 9×13-inch greased baking dish. Continue layering the remaining bread strips, cheese, bell pepper and artichoke hearts. Combine the milk, eggs, Dijon mustard, dry mustard, salt, pepper and onion in a bowl and beat well. Pour over the top of the strata. Bake at 350 degrees for 45 minutes or until lightly browned and set. Let stand for 10 minutes before serving.

Yield: 6 to 8 servings

15

16

Terri's Cheese Strata

1 loaf French bread, cubed
8 ounces cream cheese, cubed
2 1/2 cups milk
8 eggs
6 tablespoons margarine, melted
1/4 cup maple syrup
Apple Cider Sauce

Arrange 1/2 of the bread cubes in a greased 9×13-inch baking dish. Layer with the cream cheese cubes and remaining bread cubes. Combine the milk, eggs, margarine and maple syrup in a bowl and mix well. Pour over the bread and cheese layers. Chill, covered, for 8 to 10 hours. Bake, uncovered, at 325 degrees for 40 to 45 minutes or until the center is set. Let stand for a few minutes before serving. Top each serving with Apple Cider Sauce.

Yield: 8 servings

APPLE CIDER SAUCE

1/2 cup sugar
4 teaspoons cornstarch
1/2 teaspoon cinnamon
1 cup apple juice
1 teaspoon lemon juice
2 tablespoons margarine

Combine the sugar, cornstarch and cinnamon in a small saucepan. Stir in the apple juice and lemon juice. Bring to a boil over medium heat. Cook for 2 minutes or until thickened, stirring constantly. Remove the saucepan from the heat and stir in the margarine. Serve warm.

Hoosier Coffee Cake

1/3 cup packed brown sugar
1/2 cup sugar
1 teaspoon cinnamon
2 cups flour
1 teaspoon baking powder
1 teaspoon baking soda
1/2 teaspoon salt
1/2 cup (1 stick) butter, softened
1 cup sugar
2 eggs
1 teaspoon vanilla extract
1 cup sour cream

Combine the brown sugar, 1/2 cup sugar and cinnamon in a small bowl. Sift the flour, baking powder, baking soda and salt into a bowl. Cream the butter and 1 cup sugar in a large mixing bowl until light and fluffy. Beat in the eggs and vanilla. Add the flour mixture alternately with the sour cream, mixing well after each addition. Spread 1/2 of the batter in a greased 9×13-inch baking dish. Continue layering with 1/2 of the brown sugar mixture, remaining batter and remaining brown sugar mixture. Bake at 350 degrees for 20 to 30 minutes or until the coffee cake tests done.

Yield: 6 to 8 servings

Note: This recipe may be prepared ahead and refrigerated until ready to bake. It reheats well in the microwave as well.

Overnight Coffee Cake

1 (3-ounce) package vanilla cook-
 and-serve pudding mix
1/2 cup packed brown sugar
1/2 cup chopped pecans
1 (18-count) package frozen dinner
 rolls, thawed
1/2 cup (1 stick) butter, melted

Combine the pudding mix, brown sugar and pecans in a bowl. Arrange the rolls in a greased bundt pan. Pour the melted butter over the rolls and sprinkle with the pudding mixture. Let rise, covered, in a closed oven for 8 to 10 hours. Bake at 350 degrees for 30 minutes. Invert onto a serving plate.

Yield: 8 to 10 servings

Note: This is especially great if you have a programmable oven; it could be ready to eat when you wake up.

Monkey Bread

3/4 cup sugar
1 tablespoon cinnamon
4 (10-count) cans biscuits
3/4 cup (1 1/2 sticks) butter or
 margarine
1 cup sugar
Chopped nuts (optional)

Combine 3/4 cup sugar and the cinnamon in a shallow bowl. Cut each biscuit into 4 pieces; roll the pieces in the cinnamon-sugar. Arrange 1/2 of the pieces in a greased tube pan. Heat the butter and 1 cup sugar in a saucepan until the mixture comes to a boil, stirring frequently. Pour 1/2 of the butter mixture over the biscuits in the pan. Layer with the remaining biscuit pieces. Pour the remaining butter mixture over the top. Sprinkle with nuts. Bake at 325 degrees for 45 minutes. Invert onto a serving plate. Pull the bread apart into pieces to serve.

Yield: 10 to 12 servings

Sunday Morning Pancakes

3 cups flour
$1/4$ cup sugar
4 teaspoons baking powder
$1/2$ teaspoon salt
2 eggs
$2^3/4$ cups milk
$1/2$ cup vegetable oil
Apple slices, blueberries, or
*   mashed bananas (optional)*

Combine the flour, sugar, baking powder and salt in a bowl. Beat the eggs, milk and oil in a bowl. Add the egg mixture to the dry ingredients and stir just until moistened. Add fruit and stir gently. Pour $1/4$ cup of the batter at a time onto a hot lightly greased griddle. Cook until brown on both sides, turning once. Top with syrup, fruit or confectioners' sugar.

Yield: 6 servings

19

Zucchini Pancakes

$1^1/2$ cups grated zucchini,
*   squeezed dry*
2 tablespoons finely chopped onion
$1/4$ cup (1 ounce) grated Romano
*   cheese*
$1/4$ cup flour
2 eggs
2 tablespoons mayonnaise
$1/2$ teaspoon Italian seasoning
Pinch of salt
Pinch of pepper

Combine the zucchini, onion, cheese, flour, eggs, mayonnaise, Italian seasoning, salt and pepper in a bowl and mix well. Pour 2 tablespoons of the batter at a time onto a hot lightly greased griddle. Cook until brown on both sides, turning once. Serve plain or with sour cream and chives, tomato sauce or salsa.

Yield: 8 small pancakes

Note: These pancakes make a great breakfast for vegetarians.

20

Banana Bread

2 cups flour
1 teaspoon baking powder
1 teaspoon baking soda
1/2 cup margarine
1 cup sugar
2 eggs
1/2 cup buttermilk
3 medium bananas, mashed

Combine the flour, baking powder and baking soda in a bowl. Cream the margarine and sugar in a mixing bowl until light and fluffy. Beat in the eggs. Add the buttermilk and bananas and mix well. Add the dry ingredients and mix well. Pour into a greased 5×9-inch loaf pan or 4 miniature loaf pans. Bake at 325 degrees for 1 hour for the large loaf pan or 35 to 45 minutes for the small loaf pans.

Yield: 10 to 12 servings

Banana Nut Bread

2 cups sifted flour
2 teaspoons baking powder
1/2 teaspoon baking soda
3/4 teaspoon salt
1/2 cup sugar
3/4 cup chopped nuts
1 egg, beaten
1/4 cup vegetable oil
1 cup mashed bananas
1 tablespoon lemon juice
1/4 cup chopped nuts

Sift the flour, baking powder, baking soda, salt and sugar into a bowl. Stir in 3/4 cup nuts. Combine the egg, oil, bananas and lemon juice in a large bowl and mix well. Add the dry ingredients and stir just until mixed. Pour into a greased 5×9-inch loaf pan. Sprinkle with 1/4 cup nuts. Bake at 350 degrees for 45 to 50 minutes or until the loaf tests done.

Yield: 10 to 12 servings.

Sweet Blueberry Muffins

2 cups flour
1 1/2 cups sugar
2 teaspoons baking powder
1/2 cup (1 stick) butter or margarine,
    softened
2 eggs
1/2 cup milk
1 teaspoon vanilla extract
2 1/2 cups fresh or unthawed frozen
    blueberries
Sugar

Combine the flour, 1 1/2 cups sugar and baking powder in a bowl. Beat the butter in a large mixing bowl. Add the dry ingredients and mix well. Beat the eggs with the milk and vanilla in a bowl. Add to the batter and mix well. Add the blueberries, stirring gently. Fill paper-lined or greased muffin cups 1/2 full. Bake at 375 degrees for 25 to 30 minutes or until golden brown. Sprinkle the tops of the hot muffins with sugar.

Yield: 18 muffins

The Ohio Valley Athletic Conference
The largest functional athletic conference in the United States, the OVAC boasts forty-four schools in sixteen counties of Ohio and West Virginia. It covers approximately 4,500 square miles, a territory that equals half the size of New Jersey. The OVAC holds the largest track meet and conference wrestling meet in the country. To find out more about the outstanding performance of this powerhouse in the world of high school athletics, its history, and the star athletes who have graduated from it, log on to www.OVAC.org.

Carrot Cake Muffins

22

2 cups flour
1 teaspoon baking powder
1 teaspoon baking soda
1 teaspoon cinnamon
1 teaspoon salt
4 eggs
2 cups sugar
3/4 cup vegetable oil
3 cups grated peeled carrots (about
    1 pound)
1 teaspoon clear vanilla extract
1 cup chopped nuts (optional)
1 cup chopped raisins (optional)
Cream Cheese Frosting

Sift the flour, baking powder, baking soda, cinnamon and salt into a bowl. Beat the eggs, sugar, oil, carrots and vanilla in a large bowl. Add the sifted dry ingredients and stir just until moistened. Stir in the nuts and raisins. Spray muffin cups with nonstick cooking spray or line with paper liners. Fill the cups 3/4 full. Bake at 325 degrees for 24 minutes or until golden brown. Remove the muffins to a wire rack to cool. Frost the cooled muffins with Cream Cheese Frosting.

Yield: 24 muffins

Note: Clear vanilla extract is recommended for this recipe to prevent discoloration of the carrots.

CREAM CHEESE FROSTING

1/3 cup cream cheese, softened
1/4 cup (1/2 stick) butter, softened
1 teaspoon vanilla extract
2 cups confectioners' sugar
Milk

Beat the cream cheese and butter in a mixing bowl. Add the vanilla and confectioners' sugar and beat well. Add a few drops of milk if needed to make of spreading consistency.

Champagne Punch

1 bottle Champagne
1 (2-liter) bottle ginger ale, or to
    taste
1 can frozen lemonade concentrate
1 package frozen raspberries, or to
    taste

Pour the Champagne into a punch bowl. Pour in the ginger ale. Stir in the lemonade concentrate and raspberries. Serve over ice.

Yield: 8 to 10 servings

Citrus Punch

3 cups sugar
2 cups water
6 cups orange juice, chilled
6 cups grapefruit juice, chilled
1¹/₂ cups lime juice, chilled
1 (1-liter) bottle ginger ale, chilled

Bring the sugar and water to a boil in a saucepan. Cook for 5 minutes. Chill, covered, until cool. Combine the sugar syrup, orange juice, grapefruit juice and lime juice in a punch bowl. Add the ginger ale just before serving. Serve over ice.

Yield: 6 quarts

A mosaic of art created by Cross Wilkinson, Emma Blair, Haley Breski, Emily Capehart, Trey White, Lilly Barickman, Nathan Blair, Cecilia and Frankie Favede, Harrison and Anna Hartong, Sarah and Ethan McDermott, Ashley Linder, and Abby Delk. Together, these children represent the power of the imagination and creativity that was once within us all and that continues to grow in others.

Artistic Beginnings

The City of Wheeling can be proud of its vast array of opportunities available to the artist and art aficionado. The growing art community finds homes at Oglebay Institute's Stifel Fine Arts Center, Wheeling's downtown Artisan Center, and Artworks Around Town Gallery and Art Center located in Historic Centre Market. Within these halls, the youngest child or the most accomplished artist finds educational classes, gallery showings, and opportunities to market their creations.

Recognized artists are not limited to adults or professionals. Many local high school artists have been singled out locally and beyond for their creativity and discipline. It is not unusual to see their creations displayed alongside the works of the most respected professionals.

Much like our fine selection of appetizers, these young artists have a flair for beginning an artistic love affair with our area.

Stephanie Bloch

Tortilla Appetizer Wedges

8 ounces cream cheese, softened
1/2 cup sour cream
1 (4-ounce) can diced green chiles
1/2 cup sliced green onions
1 tablespoon minced red or green
*   jalapeño chile*
Salt and pepper to taste
10 (6- to 8-inch) flour tortillas
1 cup salsa, picante sauce or salsa
*   verde*

Combine the cream cheese and sour cream in a bowl and mix well. Stir in the green chiles, green onions and jalapeño chile. Add salt and pepper. Make a stack of 5 tortillas, spreading 1/4 cup of the cream cheese mixture between the tortillas. Make another stack with the remaining 5 tortillas. Wrap the stacks in plastic wrap. Chill for at least 1 hour. Cut each tortilla stack into 18 wedges. Arrange the wedges pinwheel fashion around the salsa on a serving platter.

Yield: 36 servings

Open-Face Sandwiches

*1 cup (4 ounces) shredded
   Cheddar cheese*
1 cup chopped black olives
1/3 jar bacon bits
1 cup mayonnaise
2 tablespoons chopped onion
1 package party rye bread

Combine the cheese, olives, bacon bits, mayonnaise and onion in a bowl and mix well. Spread the mixture over the bread slices. Arrange on a baking sheet. Bake at 400 degrees for 5 minutes or until bubbly.

Yield: 8 to 10 servings

Note: The spread may be prepared in advance and chilled, covered, until ready to use.

Cucumber Dainties

1 cucumber, preferably English
8 ounces cream cheese, softened
1 envelope ranch salad dressing
  mix
1 tablespoon mayonnaise
1 package party rye bread
Dill weed

29

*P*eel strips of skin at intervals around the cucumber; score the cucumber lengthwise with the tines of a fork. Slice into thin rounds. Combine the cream cheese, salad dressing mix and mayonnaise in a bowl and mix well. Spread generously over the bread slices. Top each with a slice of cucumber. Sprinkle with dill weed. Chill, covered, until serving time.

Yield: 8 to 10 servings

Miniature Bacon Puffs

8 slices bacon, crisp-cooked,
  crumbled
1 medium tomato, seeded and
  finely chopped
$^1/_2$ small onion, minced
3 ounces shredded Swiss cheese
$^1/_2$ cup mayonnaise
1 teaspoon basil (optional)
1 (10-count) can flaky biscuits

*C*ombine the bacon, tomato, onion, cheese, mayonnaise and basil in a bowl and mix well. Separate each biscuit into 3 layers. Line each of 30 miniature muffin cups with biscuit layers. Fill with the bacon mixture. Bake at 375 degrees for 10 to 12 minutes. May be prepared a day ahead, wrapped tightly and refrigerated.

Yield: 30 servings

Chicken Puffs

1 cup water
1/2 cup (1 stick) butter or margarine
1 cup flour
4 eggs
2 cups finely chopped cooked
  chicken
1/3 cup mayonnaise
1 1/2 teaspoons finely chopped onion
2 ribs celery, chopped
1 tablespoon dill weed

Bring the water and butter to a rolling boil in a 3-quart saucepan. Add the flour. Cook over low heat for 1 minute or until the mixture forms a ball, stirring vigorously. Remove from the heat. Beat in the eggs all at once; continue beating until smooth and glossy. Drop the dough by rounded teaspoonfuls onto an ungreased baking sheet. Bake at 400 degrees for 25 minutes or until puffed, golden brown and dry. Cool on a wire rack. Combine the chicken, mayonnaise, onion, celery and dill weed in a bowl and mix well. Chill, covered, before filling the puffs. Cut off the tops of the cooked puffs. Fill the puffs with the chicken mixture, then replace the tops. Chill, covered, until serving time.

Yield: 5 dozen puffs

Rumaki

1 pound chicken livers, cut into
   1-inch pieces
1 can whole water chestnuts,
   halved
Teriyaki Sauce
1 pound sliced bacon, cut into
   halves
Brown sugar

Combine the chicken livers and water chestnuts in a shallow glass bowl. Add the Teriyaki Sauce. Marinate, covered, in the refrigerator for 8 to 10 hours. Discard the marinade. Skewer 1 piece of liver and 1 water chestnut half with a wooden pick. Wrap with 1 bacon half. Repeat the procedure with the remaining liver, water chestnuts and bacon. Arrange on a baking sheet. Sprinkle with brown sugar. Bake at 350 degrees until the bacon is crisp, turning at least once.

Yield: 15 to 20 servings

Note: Drill or twist the wooden picks through the water chestnuts to keep them from splitting.

TERIYAKI SAUCE

¹/₄ cup vegetable oil
¹/₄ cup soy sauce
2 garlic cloves, crushed
2 tablespoons ketchup
1 tablespoon vinegar
¹/₄ teaspoon black, red or white
   pepper

Combine the oil, soy sauce, garlic, ketchup, vinegar and pepper in a jar and shake well.

Stuffed Mushrooms

2 ounces ham, chopped
3 tablespoons Italian dressing
3 garlic cloves, chopped
$1/2$ cup bread crumbs
$1/2$ green bell pepper, chopped
2 pounds mushroom caps

Combine the ham, Italian dressing, garlic, bread crumbs and bell pepper in a bowl and mix well. Stuff the mushroom caps with the ham mixture. Arrange in a baking pan. Bake at 400 degrees for 20 minutes.

Yield: about 20 servings

Sausage Swirls

1 (8-count) can crescent roll dough
1 pound sage bulk pork sausage

Unroll the crescent roll dough. Separate into 2 rectangles, pressing the perforations to seal. Spread each rectangle with $1/2$ of the sausage. Roll to enclose the filling. Place seam side down on a greased baking sheet. Bake at 350 degrees for 10 to 12 minutes or until sausage is cooked through. Cool slightly and cut into 1-inch slices.

Yield: 10 to 12 servings

Hummus Spread

1 large onion, chopped
1 to 2 garlic cloves, chopped
1 tablespoon olive oil
2 cups cooked chick-peas
$1/2$ cup fresh lemon juice
1 tablespoon reduced-sodium
   soy sauce
$1/4$ cup tahini
$1/2$ cup sesame seeds

Sauté the onion and garlic in the olive oil in a skillet until tender. Combine the onion mixture, chick-peas, lemon juice, soy sauce, tahini and sesame seeds in a blender or food processor and process until smooth. Serve on toasted pita bread or flatbread.

Yield: 4 to 6 servings

Hot Pepperoni Dip

16 ounces cream cheese, softened
2 cups sour cream
8 ounces pepperoni, finely chopped
$1/4$ cup chopped onion
$1/4$ cup choped green bell pepper
$1/4$ teaspoon garlic powder
$1/4$ cup French-fried onions

Combine cream cheese, sour cream, pepperoni, onion and bell pepper in a mixing bowl. Beat until well mixed. Stir in garlic powder. Spread in a pie plate. Bake at 350 degrees for 20 minutes. Sprinkle with French-fried onions. Bake for 10 minutes longer.

Yield: 10 to 15 servings

34

Pesto Pudding

24 ounces cream cheese, softened
2 eggs
1 to 1¹/₂ cups (4 to 6 ounces)
*   freshly grated Parmesan cheese*
3 to 4 tablespoons pesto

Beat the cream cheese in a mixing bowl until smooth. Add the eggs and beat until smooth and creamy. Stir in the Parmesan cheese. Spread the cream cheese mixture in a large round baking dish coated with nonstick cooking spray. Make 8 to 10 wells in the mixture, using the back of a small spoon. Fill each well with ¹/₂ to 1 teaspoon pesto. Bake at 375 degrees for 40 minutes or until golden brown. Serve warm with thin slices of crusty French bread.

Yield: 10 to 12 servings

Note: This recipe may be halved and baked in a smaller dish. Adjust the cooking time accordingly.

Black Bean Dip

1 to 2 tablespoons minced garlic
2 tablespoons olive oil
2 (16-ounce) cans black beans,
    drained
1/2 jar picante sauce (not salsa)
1/3 to 1/2 cup shredded Cheddar or
    Mexican-style cheese

35

Sauté the garlic in the olive oil in a skillet or saucepan for 1 minute. Add the black beans. Cook for 3 to 5 minutes, mashing with a fork to medium consistency. Stir in the picante sauce. Simmer for 8 to 10 minutes or until thickened. Remove to a serving dish. Add the cheese and stir until melted. Garnish with additional cheese.

Yield: 10 to 12 servings

Black Bean Salsa

1 (16-ounce) can black beans,
    drained
1 (16-ounce) can whole kernel corn,
    drained, or 2 cups fresh or frozen
    whole kernel corn
3 avocados, chopped
3 tomatoes, chopped
1 red onion, diced
1/4 cup olive oil
1/4 cup fresh lime juice
1 cup fresh cilantro, chopped

Combine the black beans, corn, avocados, tomatoes, onion, olive oil, lime juice and cilantro in a bowl and mix well. Serve with tortilla chips or as a side dish.

Yield: 10 to 12 servings

36

Championship Bean Dip

1 (16-ounce) can refried beans
1 cup picante sauce
1 cup (4 ounces) shredded
    Monterey Jack cheese
1 cup (4 ounces) shredded
    Cheddar cheese
³/4 cup sour cream
8 ounces cream cheese
1 tablespoon chili powder
¹/4 teaspoon cumin

Combine the beans, picante sauce, Monterey Jack cheese, Cheddar cheese, sour cream, cream cheese, chili powder and cumin in a slow cooker and stir well. Cook on High for 2 hours or until heated through, stirring occasionally. Serve with tortilla chips.

Yield: 10 to 12 servings

Art "Scents"

For artists young and old, try this: Mix 1 tablespoon powdered drink mix with 1 tablespoon warm water in a small container. Repeat this step with as many colors/flavors desired. Use these "paints" to create a watercolor masterpiece. Allow the painting to dry for at least eight hours. Scratch each color and sniff to release the artistic "flavor" of your work.

Spinach Artichoke Dip

1/2 cup (1 stick) margarine
2 tablespoons flour
1 cup cream
2 cups grated Parmesan cheese
2 (10-ounce) packages frozen
* chopped spinach, thawed and*
* squeezed dry*
1/2 (14-ounce) can artichoke hearts,
* chopped*
1 cup sour cream
Tabasco sauce to taste
Shredded Monterey Jack or
* Cheddar cheese*

Melt the margarine in a saucepan over medium-low heat. Whisk in the flour. Cook for 1 minute, stirring constantly. Stir in the cream and Parmesan cheese. Cook over low heat until the cheese melts, stirring constantly. Combine the spinach and artichoke hearts in a bowl and mix well. Fold in the cheese mixture, sour cream and Tabasco sauce. Remove to a greased baking dish. Top with Monterey Jack cheese. Bake at 300 degrees until bubbly. Serve with crackers or tortilla chips.

Yield: 6 to 8 servings

Cottage Cheese Dip

16 ounces cottage cheese
1 green bell pepper, finely chopped
1 red bell pepper, finely chopped
1 teaspoon garlic salt
Pepper to taste
1 envelope ranch salad dressing
  mix

Combine the cottage cheese, bell peppers, garlic salt, pepper and salad dressing mix in a bowl and mix well. Chill, covered, for at least 2 hours. Serve with crackers or breadsticks.

Yield: 8 to 10 servings

Vegetable Dip

1 cup mayonnaise
1 cup sour cream
2 tablespoons minced onion
1 tablespoon parsley flakes
1 teaspoon dill weed
1 teaspoon salt
Dash of garlic salt
Dash of pepper

Combine the mayonnaise, sour cream, onion, parsley flakes, dill weed, salt, garlic salt and pepper in a mixing bowl and beat until smooth. Chill, covered, for at least 1 hour.

Yield: 8 to 10 servings

Tortilla Chip Dip

1 cup mayonnaise
1 cup sour cream
1 envelope ranch salad dressing
    mix
2 cups (8 ounces) shredded sharp
    Cheddar cheese
2 cups (8 ounces) shredded Pepper
    Jack cheese
1 small onion, chopped or minced
1 green bell pepper, chopped
1 tomato, chopped

Combine the mayonnaise, sour cream, salad dressing mix, Cheddar cheese, Pepper Jack cheese and onion in a bowl and mix well. Remove to a serving dish. Top with the bell pepper and tomato. Serve with tortilla chips.

Yield: 10 to 12 servings

Taco Dip

8 ounces cream cheese, softened
1 cup sour cream
1 envelope taco seasoning mix
Chopped lettuce
Diced tomatoes
2 cups (8 ounces) shredded
    Cheddar cheese
1 (2-ounce) can sliced black olives

Combine the cream cheese, sour cream and taco seasoning mix in a bowl and mix well. Spread in an even layer on a flat serving dish. Layer lettuce, tomatoes, the Cheddar cheese and black olives over the cream cheese layer. Chill until serving time. Serve with tortilla chips.

Yield: 10 to 12 servings

Note: To lower the calorie count in this dip, substitute low-fat cream cheese and sour cream.

40

Hot Taco Dip

8 ounces cream cheese, softened
1 (15-ounce) can chili without beans
2 cups (8 ounces) shredded
*   Cheddar or taco cheese*

Layer the cream cheese, chili and Cheddar cheese in an 8×8-inch baking dish. Microwave on High for 2 minutes or until heated through. Serve with tortilla chips.

Yield: 10 to 12 servings

Pepperoni Dip

8 ounces cream cheese, softened
1/2 cup sour cream
1/2 cup chopped pepperoni
1/4 cup chopped green onions
1/4 cup chopped green bell pepper
1 teaspoon oregano
1/8 teaspoon garlic powder

Combine the cream cheese, sour cream, pepperoni, green onions, bell pepper, oregano and garlic powder in a bowl and mix well. Chill for at least 2 hours.

Yield: 10 to 12 servings

Easy Apple Dip

8 ounces cream cheese, softened
3/4 cup packed brown sugar
1/4 cup sugar
1 teaspoon vanilla extract
16 to 24 ounces crushed salad
   peanuts
4 to 5 apples, sliced

Combine the cream cheese, brown sugar, sugar and vanilla in a bowl and mix well. Stir in the desired amount of peanuts. Serve with the sliced apples.

Yield: 8 to 10 servings

41

CS&K Fruit Dip

8 ounces cream cheese, softened
13 ounces marshmallow creme
1 tablespoon lemon juice or orange
   juice (optional)

Combine the cream cheese and marshmallow creme in a mixing bowl and beat until smooth. Add the lemon juice and blend well. Chill until serving time. Serve with fresh fruit.

Yield: 6 to 10 servings

A Melting Pot of Flavors

Take a pinch of Lebanese, throw in a dash of German, a smidgeon of Greek, just a smattering of Irish, and mix together with an abundance of Italian, and we have ourselves a melting pot of history, culture, and great soups. Many cultural opportunities dot our cityscape the whole year through, offering a true taste of ethnic diversity while inviting everyone to taste a bit of the homelands.

Annually we celebrate Wheeling's ethnic heritage with the Celtic Celebration in early March, the African-American Jubilee in June, the Upper Ohio Valley Italian Festival in July, the American Heritage Glass & Craft Festival in August, and German food and music with the art of brewing at the German Oktoberfest in September. On a smaller, but no less popular, scale are dozens of church bazaars and fairs, county fairs, firemen's festivals, and fish fries.

Our neighbors have a flair for ethnic authenticity that is shared with everyone who experiences our area.

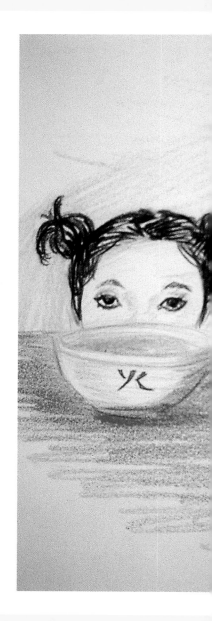

An untitled piece by Amara Carney. Amara is a college sophomore who is actively pursuing her dream of becoming a drawing professor and teaching others to excel in her favorite medium. She favors people as her subjects and hopes to continue a studio career of her own.

Chick-Pea Soup with Pasta and Pesto

2 cups chopped onions
1 cup sliced leek (1 small)
2 garlic cloves, minced
1 tablespoon chopped fresh
rosemary, or 1 teaspoon
dried rosemary
1 tablespoon olive oil
4 cups chopped tomatoes
(about 2 pounds)
3 cups water
1 (14-ounce) can fat-free low-
sodium chicken broth
1 (14-ounce) can chick-peas,
drained
1 1/2 cups frozen petite green peas
1 1/2 cups frozen French-style
green beans
1 cup diced zucchini
1/3 cup acini di pepe or other
small pasta
2 tablespoons chopped fresh
parsley (flat-leaf if available)
1/4 teaspoon pepper
2 tablespoons pesto
2 tablespoons grated Parmesan
cheese

Sauté the onions, leek, garlic and rosemary in the olive oil in a large Dutch oven over medium heat for 10 minutes. Add the tomatoes, water, chicken broth and chick-peas. Bring to a boil. Reduce the heat and simmer, covered, for 30 minutes. Add the green peas, green beans and zucchini. Bring to a boil. Reduce the heat and simmer for 10 minutes. Stir in the pasta, parsley and pepper. Cook for 8 minutes longer. Ladle 1 1/2 cups soup into each of 6 bowls. Garnish each serving with 1 teaspoon pesto and 1 teaspoon cheese.

Yield: 6 servings

45

Greek Chicken Soup

1 (4-pound) chicken, cut up
4 quarts water
2 medium onions, quartered
4 ribs celery
1¹/₂ teaspoons salt, or to taste
¹/₂ teaspoon pepper
³/₄ cup rice (or any fine pasta such
    as angel hair)
Egg Lemon Sauce

Combine the chicken, water, onions and celery in a soup pot. Bring to a boil. Reduce the heat and simmer for 1¹/₂ to 2 hours or until the chicken is tender, adding the salt and pepper halfway through cooking time. Remove the chicken and reserve for another use. Strain the broth. Bring the broth back to a boil. Stir in the rice and cook over medium heat until tender. Beat a small amount of the hot broth into the Egg Lemon Sauce. Continue beating in small amounts of hot broth until Egg Lemon Sauce is hot. Pour all of the sauce into the soup pot, stirring constantly. The top of the soup should be foamy. Serve immediately.

Yield: 8 to 10 servings

Note: Add some of the cooked chicken to the soup bowls if desired. Or brush pieces of the chicken with melted butter and brown them in the oven.

EGG LEMON SAUCE

4 eggs, at room temperature
Juice of 1¹/₂ lemons, or to taste

Beat the eggs at high speed in a mixing bowl until thick and pale yellow. Add the lemon juice, beating constantly.

Chicken Rice Soup

1 (2- to 3-pound) chicken or
  chicken pieces
2 teaspoons salt
2 onions, quartered
2 carrots, quartered
2 ribs celery with leaves
2 teaspoons salt
1 teaspoon cinnamon
3 tablespoons minced parsley
1 teaspoon pepper
3 ounces tomato paste, or 4 ounces
  tomato sauce
1/2 cup rice

Rinse the chicken and remove extra fat. Rub the chicken with 1 teaspoon salt. Combine the chicken, enough water to cover and 1 teaspoon salt in a soup pot. Bring to a boil. Reduce the heat and simmer, skimming foam from the surface. Stir in the onions, carrots, celery, 2 teaspoons salt, cinnamon, parsley and pepper. Simmer, partially covered, for 1 hour, turning the chicken occasionally. Remove the chicken. Let stand until cool enough to handle. Chop the chicken, discarding the skin and bones. Strain the broth. Chop the vegetables and add to the broth or discard. Add the chicken and tomato paste. Bring to a boil. Rinse and drain the rice and stir into the soup. Adjust seasonings. Reduce the heat and simmer for 30 minutes or until the rice is tender.

Yield: 4 to 8 servings

47

48

Tortilla Soup

2 (10-ounce) cans chicken and
    rice soup
1 large can, or 3 small cans,
    chicken broth
1 (14-ounce) can diced tomatoes
1 (4-ounce) can chopped green
    chiles
4 ounces drained canned whole
    kernel corn
1 onion, chopped
2 garlic cloves, minced
Crumbled tortilla chips
Chopped tomatoes
Chopped avocado
Shredded Cheddar or Monterey
    Jack cheese

Combine the soup, chicken broth, diced tomatoes, green chiles, corn, onion and garlic in a soup pot. Bring to a boil. Ladle the soup into bowls filled with chips, chopped tomatoes, avocado and cheese.

Yield: 6 to 8 servings

Slow Cooker Stuffed Pepper Soup

2 pounds lean ground beef
1 green bell pepper, chopped
2 beef bouillon cubes
1 cup boiling water
37 ounces tomato sauce
1 (29-ounce) can diced tomatoes
1/4 cup packed brown sugar
2 teaspoons salt
1 teaspoon pepper
1 tablespoon soy sauce
2 cups cooked rice

Brown the ground beef in a skillet, stirring until crumbly; drain. Add the bell pepper and sauté for 5 minutes. Remove the ground beef mixture to a slow cooker. Dissolve the bouillon cubes in the boiling water. Stir the bouillon, tomato sauce, diced tomatoes, brown sugar, salt, pepper and soy sauce into the ground beef mixture. Cook on High for 6 to 7 hours, stirring occasionally and adding the rice 1 hour before the end of the cooking time.

Yield: 10 servings

Elwood's Ham Chowder

2 pounds country ham, coarsely
    ground or minced
2 tablespoons vegetable oil
6 cups diced onions
4 tablespoons sliced garlic cloves
1 1/2 gallons collard greens, washed,
    stemmed and chopped
1 (35-ounce) can whole tomatoes,
    chopped
3 1/2 quarts chicken stock
32 ounces beef stock
3 quarts red potatoes, cut into
    1/4-inch cubes
3 tablespoons thyme
3 tablespoons parsley
Salt to taste
1 tablespoon pepper
2 tablespoons Tabasco sauce

Cook the ham in the oil in a large soup pot over low heat to slowly render the fat. Do not allow the ham to brown. Add the onions and garlic. Cook over low heat until the onions and garlic are tender, adding additional oil if necessary. Add the collard greens in batches, stirring as they wilt. Add the undrained tomatoes, chicken stock, beef stock, potatoes, thyme, parsley, salt, pepper and Tabasco sauce and mix well. Bring to a boil. Reduce the heat and simmer for 20 to 30 minutes or until the potatoes are cooked through, stirring occasionally. Skim the surface of any foam or oil that appears during cooking.

Yield: 3 gallons

Note: This recipe is from Magnolia's Uptown/Down South, Blossom Café, and Cypress.

49

Donald Barickman is the brother-in-law of one of our League members and is the executive chef and partner of three restaurants in Charleston, South Carolina: Magnolia's, Blossom Café, and Cypress. Chef Barickman is a native West Virginian and was trained at the Culinary Institute of America in New York. Also, Chef Barickman has been featured in national publications such as Bon Appétit, Southern Living, *and* Martha Stewart Living, *to name a few. This recipe was developed with his father and is just one of his many culinary treasures.*

Cheese Soup

5 slices bacon
$^1/_2$ cup grated carrots
$^1/_2$ cup finely chopped onion
$^1/_2$ cup finely chopped celery
$^1/_2$ cup finely chopped green bell
   pepper
$^1/_4$ cup flour
4 cups chicken broth
3 cups (12 ounces) shredded
   Cheddar cheese or Velveeta
   cheese
2 cups milk
2 tablespoons dry sherry
Pepper to taste
Fresh parsley, chopped

Cook the bacon in a skillet until crisp; drain, reserving the drippings. Crumble the bacon. Sauté the carrots, onion, celery and bell pepper in the bacon drippings over low heat until tender but not browned. Stir in the flour. Add the chicken broth gradually, stirring constantly. Cook over low heat until the mixture thickens. Cook for 5 minutes longer. Add the cheese and stir until melted. Stir in the milk and sherry. Heat the soup to just below boiling. Season with pepper. Ladle the soup into bowls and garnish with the crumbled bacon and parsley.

Yield: 2 quarts

Note: This recipe may be doubled and freezes well.

50

Do You Speak Soup?

Make a lasting impression at dinner tonight. Serve an ethnic dish with the flair of the motherland. Good soup is good in any language!

Σούπα—Greek	Sopa—Spanish	Tang—Chinese	Soppa—Swedish
Suppe—German	Anraith—Irish	Zupa—Polish	Ius—Latin
Soupe—French	Cyп—Russian	Soep—Dutch	He supa—Hawaiian
Minestra—Italian	Leves—Hungarian	Kuk—Korean	Supo—Esperanto

Broccoli Soup

3 large stalks broccoli
1 medium onion, chopped
1 rib celery, chopped
1 medium carrot, chopped
3 tablespoons butter
3 cups chicken broth or vegetable
   broth
1¹/₂ cups half-and-half
Salt and pepper to taste

Remove the crowns from the broccoli stalks and separate into florets; chop the stalks coarsely. Sauté the onion, celery and carrots in the butter in a soup pot until golden brown. Add the chopped broccoli stalks and the chicken broth. Bring to a boil. Reduce the heat and simmer for 15 minutes. Add the broccoli florets, reserving a few for garnish. Cook for 5 minutes. Purée the soup in a blender, 2 cups at a time. Stir in the half-and-half, salt and pepper. Heat to just below boiling to serve hot. Chill for at least 4 hours to serve cold.

Yield: 8 servings

51

Cauliflower Soup

²/₃ cup chopped onion
¹/₄ cup (¹/₂ stick) butter
¹/₄ cup flour
2 cups chicken broth
1 head cauliflower, chopped
2 cups light cream
¹/₂ teaspoon Worcestershire sauce
³/₄ teaspoon salt
1 cup (4 ounces) shredded
   Cheddar cheese
Pepper to taste
Fresh chives, minced

Sauté the onion in the butter in a soup pot until tender. Stir in the flour. Add the chicken broth and cook until thickened, stirring constantly. Add the cauliflower, cream, Worcestershire sauce and salt. Cook until the cauliflower is tender. Remove from the heat and stir in the cheese and pepper. Ladle the soup into bowls and garnish with chives.

Yield: 8 to 10 servings

Lentil Noodle Soup

8 cups water
1 teaspoon salt
1 cup lentils, rinsed and drained
2 small onions, chopped
1 garlic clove, or 1 teaspoon garlic
*   extract*
2 tablespoons ground or crushed
*   coriander (optional)*
$1/2$ cup vegetable oil
3 cups egg noodles
2 tablespoons butter

Bring the water and salt to a boil in a soup pot. Stir in the lentils. Simmer, partially covered, until tender. Sauté the onions, garlic and coriander in the oil in a skillet until brown, stirring frequently. Discard the garlic if desired. Add the onion mixture, including the oil, to the lentils. Stir in the noodles and butter. Bring to a boil. Reduce the heat and simmer until the noodles are tender, stirring occasionally. Check the seasonings. Serve the soup hot or cold.

Yield: 4 to 6 servings

Lentil Rice Soup

6 cups water
1 teaspoon salt
1 cup lentils, rinsed and drained
2 medium onions, finely chopped
1/2 teaspoon minced garlic
1/2 cup vegetable oil
1/2 cup rice, rinsed and drained

Bring the water and salt to a boil in a soup pot. Stir in the lentils. Simmer, partially covered, until tender. Crush some of the lentils on the side of the pot to thicken the soup. Sauté the onions and garlic in the oil in a skillet until brown, stirring frequently. Add the onion mixture, including the oil, to the lentils. Season as desired. Add the rice and simmer over low heat until tender. The soup will be very thick. Serve hot or at room temperature.

Yield: 4 servings

53

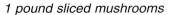

Mushroom Soup

1 pound sliced mushrooms
1 medium onion, sliced
1 teaspoon garlic salt
2 tablespoons olive oil
2 tablespoons butter
3 tablespoons tomato paste
3 cups chicken broth
2 ounces dry vermouth
1/4 cup freshly grated Parmesan
   cheese
1/2 cup chopped fresh parsley
3 egg yolks

54

Sauté the mushrooms, onion and garlic salt in the olive oil and butter in a soup pot for 15 minutes. Add the tomato paste, chicken broth and dry vermouth. Simmer for 15 minutes. Combine the cheese, parsley and egg yolks in a small bowl. Whisk 1/2 cup of the soup into the cheese mixture and stir the mixture back into the soup. Heat to just below boiling or the eggs will curdle.

Yield: 4 servings

Note: If you like the flavor of garlic, add 1 tablespoon garlic powder.

Finnegan's Irish Cream Potato Soup

6 large baking potatoes
5 (10-ounce) cans cream of
 celery soup
2 tablespoons butter
1 teaspoon garlic salt
1/2 teaspoon salt
1/2 teaspoon crushed red pepper
1/2 teaspoon black pepper
Milk
2 teaspoons minced garlic
1 large white onion, diced
2 cups (8 ounces) shredded or
 diced mild Cheddar cheese
1 teaspoon sugar
Bacon bits

Combine the potatoes with enough water to cover in a soup pot. Bring to a boil. Boil until tender; drain. Mash the potatoes in the pot. Add the celery soup and mash again. Add the butter, garlic salt, salt, red pepper and black pepper. Beat with a hand mixer while adding enough milk to make of the desired consistency. Stir in the minced garlic, onion, cheese and sugar. Simmer for 30 minutes. Ladle the soup into bowls and garnish with bacon bits.

Yield: 10 to 12 servings

55

Tortellini Chowder

1 medium onion, chopped
1 red bell pepper, chopped
1 Anaheim, poblano or jalapeño
   chile, seeded and chopped
   (about 1 tablespoon)
3 garlic cloves, minced
2 tablespoons butter
3 (14-ounce) cans vegetable broth
3 cups cubed peeled potatoes
1 1/2 teaspoons cumin
1/2 teaspoon salt
1/2 teaspoon black pepper
1/4 teaspoon ground red pepper
3 tablespoons flour
3 tablespoons butter, melted
1 (15-ounce) can whole kernel
   corn, drained
3 cups half-and-half
2 (16-ounce) packages frozen
   cheese tortellini, thawed in
   refrigerator
Corn tortilla strips or broken
   tortilla chips

Cook the onion, bell pepper, Anaheim chile and garlic in 2 tablespoons butter in a large soup pot until the vegetables are tender but not brown. Stir in the vegetable broth, potatoes, cumin, salt, black pepper and red pepper. Bring to a boil. Reduce the heat and simmer, covered, for 25 to 30 minutes or until the potatoes are tender. Blend the flour and the melted butter in a small bowl; add to the soup mixture. Cook over medium heat until thickened and bubbly, stirring constantly. Cook for 1 minute, stirring constantly. Reduce the heat. Add the corn, half-and-half and tortellini. Cook until heated through. Ladle the soup into bowls and top with tortilla strips or broken tortilla chips.

Yield: 6 to 8 servings

Vegetarian Chili

2 cups finely chopped onions
3/4 cup chopped celery
1 cup chopped green bell pepper
1 cup chopped carrots
1 tablespoon minced garlic
2 cups chopped mushrooms
2 tablespoons chili powder
1 tablespoon cumin
3/4 teaspoon basil
3/4 teaspoon oregano
1/4 teaspoon red pepper flakes
2 teaspoons salt
1/2 teaspoon black pepper
1/3 cup olive oil
1 (20-ounce) can kidney beans
3/4 cup bulgur
2 tablespoons chopped green
   chiles, or to taste
2 cups (or more) tomato juice
2 cups chopped tomatoes
3 tablespoons tomato paste
1/2 teaspoon Tabasco sauce
2 tablespoons lemon juice
1 tablespoon Worcestershire sauce
1/4 cup dry red wine or dry white
   wine

Cook the onions, celery, bell pepper, carrots, garlic, mushrooms, chili powder, cumin, basil, oregano, red pepper flakes, salt and black pepper in the olive oil in a soup pot over high heat for 1 to 2 minutes, stirring constantly. Stir in the undrained kidney beans. Add the bulgur, green chiles, tomato juice, tomatoes, tomato paste, Tabasco sauce, lemon juice, Worcestershire sauce and wine. Bring to a boil, stirring constantly. Reduce the heat. Simmer for 20 minutes. Thin the soup with additional tomato juice if needed.

Yield: 4 to 6 servings

Note: Bulgur consists of dried wheat kernels and is a nutritious substitute for meat in this soup. To make preparation easier, chop all the vegetables in a food processor.

57

Stroll the Garden Path

In the mid-1920s, the City of Wheeling was the recipient of two land holdings that have become recreation areas unsurpassed anywhere in the scope of their facilities and programs. Wheeling Park, saved from urban development in 1923 by the foresight of local businessmen and purchased through the philanthropic efforts of over 170 local citizens, has grown into a 450-acre community recreation area.

In 1926, Colonel E. W. Oglebay willed his beautiful country estate, Waddington Farms, to the City of Wheeling for recreation and educational purposes. Today, Oglebay is a 1,600-acre resort shared with visitors from every state and many foreign countries.

These parks offer their visitors many paths to stroll while enjoying the landscape. Wheeling and Oglebay Parks have more than just scenery. People can enjoy everything from tennis to fishing, miniature golf, and ice-skating. Picnic shelters offer daily respites as well as sites in which to celebrate. Museums, shopping, and theaters add to the list of recreation. Oglebay also boasts a small fully accredited zoo.

The Ohio Valley certainly adds flair to strolling the outdoors. Residents have the same creativity with their salad recipes, bringing a bit of the great outdoors inside, no matter the season.

"Oglebay Garden Path" by Pat Temple. Mrs. Temple, originally from Rochester, New York, proclaims that she became a photographer by chance. She has shot beautiful scenery and wildlife in locations ranging from local nature camps to South America and Europe.

June Paull

Couscous Salad with Dried Cherries

1 cup chicken broth
3/4 cup couscous
1/2 cup dried cherries
1/2 cup coarsely chopped carrots
1/2 cup chopped unpeeled
   cucumber
1/4 cup thinly sliced scallions
1/4 cup pine nuts
Balsamic Vinaigrette
Salt and pepper to taste

Bring the chicken broth to a boil in a medium saucepan. Stir in the couscous. Remove from the heat and let stand, covered, for 5 minutes. Fluff with a fork and let cool, uncovered, for 10 minutes. Combine the couscous, dried cherries, carrots, cucumber, scallions and pine nuts in a salad bowl. Add the Balsamic Vinaigrette, salt and pepper and mix well. Chill until serving time.

Yield: 6 to 8 servings

61

BALSAMIC VINAIGRETTE

3 tablespoons balsamic vinegar
1 tablespoon olive oil
1 tablespoon Dijon mustard

Whisk the vinegar, olive oil and Dijon mustard in a small bowl.

Hot Chicken Salad

1 cup chopped cooked chicken
1 cup cooked rice
1 cup chopped celery
1 (10-ounce) can cream of chicken
    soup
³/4 cup sliced almonds or water
    chestnuts
¹/4 cup light mayonnaise
2 tablespoons chopped onion
Crushed cornflakes
Butter

Combine the chicken, rice, celery, cream of chicken soup, almonds, mayonnaise and onion in an 8×8-inch baking dish. Top with crushed cornflakes and dot with butter. Bake at 350 degrees for 45 minutes.

Yield: 4 servings

Chicken and Bow Tie Pasta Salad

1 head broccoli, cut into pieces
16 ounces bow tie pasta
1 pound grilled chicken breasts,
    sliced
3/4 cup chopped fresh basil
White Wine Vinaigrette
1 pint cherry tomatoes, halved
16 ounces torn romaine

Steam the broccoli until tender-crisp; drain and chill. Cook the pasta in boiling salted water in a large saucepan just until tender. Rinse under cold water and drain. Combine the broccoli, pasta, chicken, basil and White Wine Vinaigrette in a salad bowl and mix well. Chill for at least 4 hours. Add the tomatoes and romaine and toss well.

Yield: 10 to 12 servings

WHITE WINE VINAIGRETTE

63

2/3 cup vegetable oil
1/4 cup white wine vinegar
1/4 cup water
1 tablespoon salt
1 tablespoon pepper
2 garlic cloves, minced

Whisk the oil, vinegar, water, salt, pepper and garlic in a small bowl.

Chick-Pea Macaroni Salad

1 cup macaroni
1 (19-ounce) can chick-peas,
   drained
4 tomatoes, chopped
1 onion, chopped
6 ounces feta cheese, crumbled
1 cup pitted black olives
1/2 cup olive oil
1/4 cup fresh lemon juice
1 garlic clove, minced
1 teaspoon salt
1/2 teaspoon pepper

Cook the pasta in boiling salted water in a large saucepan just until tender. Rinse under cold water and drain. Combine the pasta, chick-peas, tomatoes, onion, cheese, black olives, olive oil, lemon juice, garlic, salt and pepper in a salad bowl and mix well. Chill until serving time.

Yield: 4 to 6 servings

Note: This Greek-style pasta is also good tossed with fresh avocado and mint.

64

Green Bean, Walnut and Feta Salad

2 pounds green beans, trimmed
   and cut diagonally into thirds
1/2 small Bermuda onion, thinly
   sliced
4 ounces feta cheese, crumbled
1 cup toasted walnuts, coarsely
   chopped
Dill Vinaigrette

Cook the green beans in boiling salted water in a large saucepan until tender-crisp; drain. Immediately plunge the green beans into a large bowl filled with ice water; drain and pat dry. Combine the beans, onion, cheese and walnuts in a salad bowl. Chill, covered, for 1 hour. Pour the Dill Vinaigrette over the bean mixture and toss. Chill for at least 1 hour before serving.

Yield: 6 to 8 servings

Note: This is a great side dish for a luncheon.

65

DILL VINAIGRETTE

3/4 cup extra-virgin olive oil
1/4 cup red wine vinegar or white
   wine vinegar
1 tablespoon chopped fresh dill
   weed
1/2 teaspoon minced garlic
1/2 teaspoon salt
1/4 teaspoon pepper

Whisk the olive oil, vinegar, dill weed, garlic, salt and pepper in a small bowl. Chill for 1 hour.

Chinese Salad

¹/₂ cup vegetable oil
¹/₄ cup red wine vinegar
¹/₂ cup sugar
1 tablespoon soy sauce
¹/₂ cup slivered almonds
¹/₂ package ramen noodles,
   crushed
1 head Chinese celery cabbage,
   shredded

Whisk the oil, vinegar, sugar and soy sauce in a small bowl. Chill for 8 to 10 hours. Combine the almonds and ramen noodles on a baking sheet. Bake at 325 degrees for 5 minutes or until light brown. Combine the cabbage, almond mixture and oil and vinegar dressing in a salad bowl and mix well.

Yield: 4 to 6 servings

Day-Ahead Salad

1 large red onion, sliced into rings
1 head cauliflower, chopped
1 crown broccoli, chopped
1 pint cherry tomatoes, halved
1 (10-ounce) package frozen peas
2 cups mayonnaise
1 envelope ranch salad dressing
   mix
Salt and pepper to taste

Combine the onion, caulifower, broccoli, cherry tomatoes and peas in a mixing bowl. Whisk the mayonnaise and salad dressing mix in a small bowl. Stir into the vegetables. Add salt and pepper. Remove to a large shallow serving dish. Marinate, covered, in the refrigerator for 8 to 10 hours.

Yield: 8 to 10 servings

Broccoli Salad Supreme

1¹/₂ large crowns broccoli,
    separated into florets
1 pound bacon, crisp-cooked and
    crumbled
1 small to medium red onion, finely
    chopped
1 cup mayonnaise
¹/₂ cup sugar
2 tablespoons vinegar
2 cups (8 ounces) shredded
    mozzarella cheese

Combine the broccoli, bacon, and onion in a salad bowl. Combine the mayonnaise, sugar and vinegar in a bowl and mix well. Spoon over the broccoli mixture and toss to mix. Sprinkle with the cheese. Chill for a few hours before serving.

Yield: 6 to 8 servings

67

Red Dill Potato Salad

3 pounds small red potatoes
1 small red bell pepper, diced
1 small yellow bell pepper, diced
¹/₂ cup mayonnaise
¹/₂ cup sour cream
2 tablespoons grainy mustard
1 bunch fresh dill weed, chopped
Salt and lemon pepper to taste

Slice the potatoes. Combine the potatoes with enough water to cover in a saucepan. Bring to a boil. Boil until tender; drain and cool. Combine the bell peppers, mayonnaise, sour cream, grainy mustard, dill weed, salt and lemon pepper in a bowl and stir well. Fold into the potatoes in a salad bowl. Chill until serving time.

Yield: 4 servings

My Grandma's German Potato Salad

6 to 8 large potatoes
6 slices bacon
1 small onion, minced
1 tablespoon pickle relish
1 teaspoon celery seeds
2 to 3 tablespoons flour
2 tablespoons sugar
1/2 cup cider vinegar

Combine the potatoes with enough water to cover in a saucepan. Bring to a boil. Boil until tender; drain and peel. Cut into 1-inch cubes. Cook the bacon in a skillet until crisp; drain, reserving the drippings. Crumble the bacon. Combine the bacon, onion, pickle relish and celery seeds in a bowl and mix well. Spoon over the potatoes in a salad bowl. Heat the bacon drippings in the skillet. Stir in enough of the flour to make a roux. Add the sugar and vinegar. Cook for 2 minutes or until thickened, stirring constantly. Pour the dressing over the potatoes and stir well. Let the salad marinate until serving time. Serve warm or at room temperature.

Yield: 6 to 8 servings

Mustard Dill Potato Salad

2 pounds red potatoes
2 hard-cooked eggs, chopped
1/2 cup finely chopped celery
1/3 cup finely chopped red onion
1/2 cup chopped fresh dill weed
1/2 cup mayonnaise
1 tablespoon white wine vinegar
1 tablespoon Dijon mustard
Salt and pepper to taste

Cut the potatoes into chunks. Combine with enough salted water to cover in a saucepan. Bring to a boil. Boil until tender; drain and cool. Combine the potatoes, eggs, celery, onion and dill weed in a salad bowl. Combine the mayonnaise, vinegar and Dijon mustard in a small bowl and mix well. Fold into the potato mixture. Add salt and pepper. Chill until serving time.

Yield: 8 to 10 servings

69

Caesar Salad Dressing

1/2 cup mayonnaise
1/4 cup olive oil
1/4 cup grated Parmesan cheese
1 garlic clove, pressed
3 tablespoons lemon juice
1 teaspoon Worcestershire sauce
Salt and pepper to taste

Combine the mayonnaise, olive oil, cheese, garlic, lemon juice, Worcestershire sauce, salt and pepper in a jar with a tight-fitting lid and shake well. Chill until serving time.

Yield: 1 cup

Mixed Greens with Goat Cheese Crostini

4 ounces goat cheese, softened
1 baguette, cut diagonally into
  1-inch slices
8 cups mixed salad greens
3 tablespoons pine nuts, toasted
Sun-Dried Tomato Vinaigrette
Salt and pepper to taste

Spread 1 tablespoon goat cheese over each baguette slice. Arrange the slices on a baking sheet. Combine the salad greens, pine nuts, Sun-Dried Tomato Vinaigrette, salt and pepper in a salad bowl and toss. Divide among 4 salad plates. Broil the prepared baguette slices for 1 minute or until the cheese just begins to melt. Top each salad with 2 crostini.

Yield: 4 servings

70

SUN-DRIED TOMATO VINAIGRETTE

$1/2$ cup virgin olive oil
$1/4$ cup red wine vinegar
3 tablespoons chopped drained
  oil-packed sun-dried tomatoes
2 small garlic cloves, minced

Whisk the olive oil, vinegar, sun-dried tomatoes and garlic in a small bowl.

Spinach Salad with Strawberries

10 ounces fresh spinach
1 pint strawberries, sliced
1 cup chopped celery
$^1/_2$ cup sliced almonds
Green Onion Dressing

inse and dry the spinach. Remove and discard the stems. Tear the leaves into a large salad bowl. Add the strawberries, celery and almonds and toss. Pour the desired amount of the Green Onion Dressing over the salad before serving.

Yield: 8 to 10 servings

GREEN ONION DRESSING

3 green onions, chopped
2 cups vegetable oil
$^2/_3$ cup vinegar
$^1/_2$ cup sugar
2 teaspoons dry mustard
2 teaspoons salt

Combine the green onions, oil, vinegar, sugar, dry mustard and salt in a jar with a tight-fitting lid and shake well. Chill until serving time.

The Well-Dressed Salad
Here are two more easy-to-make dressings to enjoy with your salad greens.

Poppy Seed Dressing: *Combine $^1/_2$ cup sugar, $^1/_2$ cup cider vinegar, 3 tablespoons chopped onion, $^1/_2$ teaspoon paprika and $^1/_4$ teaspoon Worcestershire sauce in a blender and process until smooth. Add $^1/_2$ cup vegetable oil and 1 teaspoon poppy seeds and process until well blended. Store the dressing in the refrigerator. Yield: about 1 cup.*

Caesar Salad Dressing: *Combine 1 cup vegetable oil, 1 cup grated Parmesan cheese, the juice of 1 lemon, 2 crushed garlic cloves, $^1/_2$ teaspoon Worcestershire sauce and $^1/_2$ teaspoon prepared mustard in a bowl and mix well. Optional additions are 2 anchovies and 1 uncooked pasteurized egg. Store the dressing in the refrigerator. Serve over romaine. Yield: about $1^1/_2$ cups.*

Colorful Tossed Salad

Grape Juice Vinaigrette
10 cups mixed salad greens
8 large strawberries, quartered
1 kiwifruit, sliced
2 tablespoons sliced green onions
2 tablespoons chopped macadamia
    nuts, toasted

Reserve 2 tablespoons of the Grape Juice Vinaigrette. Combine the salad greens and remaining Grape Juice Vinaigrette in a salad bowl and toss to mix. Top with the strawberries, kiwifruit and green onions. Drizzle with the reserved dressing. Sprinkle with the nuts.

Yield: 8 servings

GRAPE JUICE VINAIGRETTE

$1/4$ cup white grape juice
    concentrate
3 tablespoons cider vinegar
2 teaspoons canola oil
$1/2$ teaspoon salt
$1/4$ teaspoon onion powder

Combine the grape juice concentrate, vinegar, canola oil, salt and onion powder in a jar with a tight-fitting lid and shake well. Chill until serving time.

Coca-Cola Salad

*1 (15-ounce) can pitted black
   cherries
1 (20-ounce) can crushed pineapple
1 (3-ounce) package black cherry
   gelatin
1 (3-ounce) package strawberry
   gelatin
26 ounces Coca-Cola
9 ounces cream cheese
1 cup chopped nuts*

Drain the cherries and pineapple, reserving the juices. Combine the juices in a saucepan and bring to a boil. Pour over the black cherry and strawberry gelatin in a large bowl, stirring until dissolved. Add the Coca-Cola. Combine the cream cheese and nuts in a large bowl. Add the gelatin mixture to the cream cheese mixture, stirring until smooth. Pour into a 9×13-inch dish. Chill until set.

Yield: 8 to 10 servings

73

Don't Forget the Sides

The Ohio Valley is very proud of its history. We savor the past by remembering the industries that made this area famous.

We celebrate the steel and nail industries and the founders who introduced them to a young nation. A pioneer industry with an unbroken record of success, the manufacturing of nails began in Wheeling, West Virginia, in 1834. With nails being one of Wheeling's leading products, the nickname "Nail City" came naturally.

Industry leaders, Fenton Glass, Fostoria, and Imperial, were the heart of the glass industry in the United States beginning in 1887, putting fancy glass on tables and shelves across the country.

The stogie business could not be mentioned at all without mentioning the Marsh-Wheeling brand. The Marsh-Wheeling Stogie has been synonymous with the tobacco industry since 1886, and although out of business, it is still recognized today. The insignia still adorns the Wheeling cityscape as a great reminder and mainstay.

Sharing the past adds flair to the future...like a good side dish adds flair to any entrée.

"Wheeling-Pittsburgh Steel Building" by Anne Foreman. Mrs. Foreman has lived in Wheeling all her life and has raised six children here as well. She explains that she "dabbled" in art classes over the years, but that it "was some 30 years later that her art career gained momentum and her passion took flight!" She "hopes it takes her into the next 35 years."

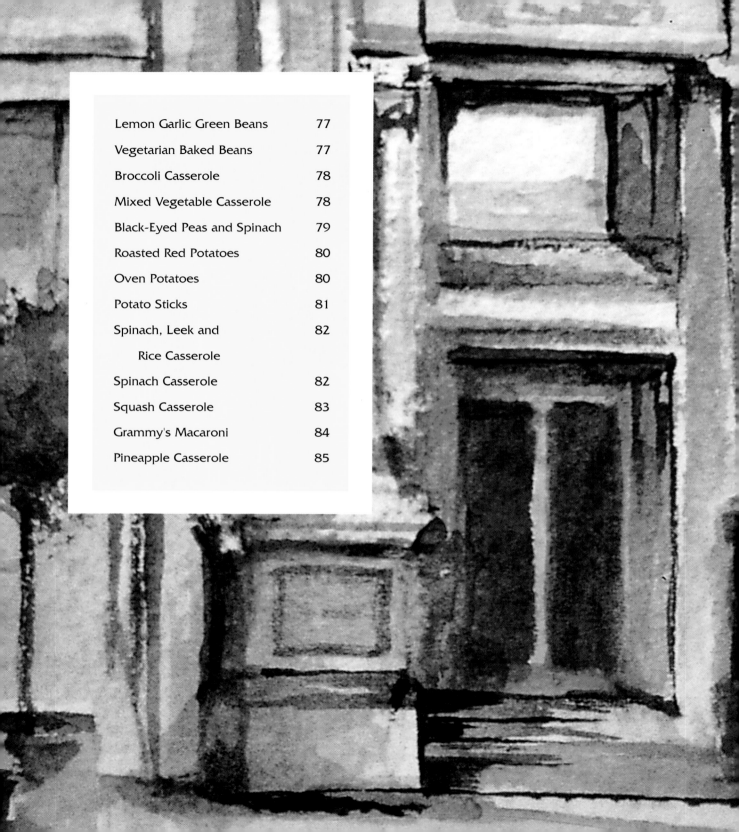

Lemon Garlic Green Beans

1 pound green beans, trimmed
1/2 teaspoon salt
1 cup boiling water
3 garlic cloves, minced
2 tablespoons vegetable oil
1 teaspoon grated lemon zest
3 tablespoons lemon juice
1/2 teaspoon pepper

Add the beans and salt to the water in a saucepan. Boil, covered, for 10 minutes; drain. Sauté the garlic in the oil in a skillet for 1 to 2 minutes, stirring constantly. Add the beans, lemon zest, lemon juice and pepper and stir well.

Yield: 4 servings

Vegetarian Baked Beans

2 (16-ounce) cans vegetarian
    baked beans in tomato sauce
2 (16-ounce) cans barbecue beans
1 cup tomato sauce
1/2 cup chopped onion
2 tablespoons margarine
2 tablespoons molasses or brown
    sugar
2 teaspoons dry mustard

Combine the baked beans, barbecue beans, tomato sauce, onion, margarine, molasses and dry mustard in a bowl and mix well. Spoon into a 3-quart baking dish. Bake at 350 degrees for 45 to 60 minutes.

Yield: 8 to 12 servings

Note: Double the recipe for a crowd. Add 30 to 40 minutes to the baking time.

77

Broccoli Casserole

2 (16-ounce) packages frozen
   chopped broccoli
12 ounces Velveeta cheese, diced
$1/2$ cup (1 stick) butter or margarine,
   cut into chunks
2 sleeves butter crackers, crushed
$1/4$ cup ($1/2$ stick) butter or
   margarine, cut into chunks

Cook the broccoli using the package directions; drain. Combine the broccoli, cheese and $1/2$ cup butter in a bowl and mix well. Spoon into a buttered 9×13-inch baking dish. Top with the cracker crumbs and $1/4$ cup butter. Bake at 350 degrees for 30 minutes or until bubbly.

Yield: 10 servings

Note: Fresh broccoli may be substituted for the frozen broccoli.

Mixed Vegetable Casserole

1 (10-ounce) package frozen mixed
   vegetables
$1/2$ cup chopped celery
$1/2$ cup chopped onion
$1/2$ cup mayonnaise
$1/2$ cup (4 ounces) shredded
   Cheddar cheese
20 saltines, crushed
Butter, melted

Combine the mixed vegetables, celery, onion, mayonnaise and cheese in a bowl and mix well. Spoon into an 8×8-inch baking dish. Combine the cracker crumbs and a small amount of butter in a bowl and mix well. Sprinkle evenly over the vegetable mixture. Bake at 350 degrees for 30 minutes.

Yield: 8 to 10 servings

Black-Eyed Peas and Spinach

4 to 6 slices bacon
1 medium onion, chopped
2 (10-ounce) packages frozen
  black-eyed peas, thawed
1 (10-ounce) can chicken broth
Salt to taste
Pepper or Cajun seasoning to taste
10 ounces fresh spinach, torn and
  stems removed

Cook the bacon in a Dutch oven until crisp. Remove the bacon, reserving 2 tablespoons drippings; drain. Crumble the bacon. Sauté the onion in the drippings until tender. Add the black-eyed peas and chicken broth. Bring to a boil. Reduce the heat and simmer, covered, until the peas are almost tender, stirring frequently and adding water as needed. Stir in the bacon, salt and pepper. Cook until the peas are tender, adding additional water as needed. Stir in the spinach. Cook, covered, for 3 to 5 minutes.

Yield: 6 to 8 servings

Note: Make this dish a day ahead if you wish. When you reheat, add water to thin if needed.

79

Roasted Red Potatoes

3½ pounds medium-size red
   potatoes, quartered
1 medium onion, chopped
2 tablespoons olive oil
2 teaspoons rosemary
2 teaspoons salt
¾ teaspoon pepper

Combine the potatoes, onion, olive oil, rosemary, salt and pepper in a bowl and mix well. Spoon into a baking dish. Roast at 400 degrees for 40 to 45 minutes, stirring once halfway through the cooking time.

Yield: 4 to 6 servings

Oven Potatoes

2 to 3 pounds white or red potatoes,
   cut as for French fries
1 teaspoon seasoned salt
½ teaspoon pepper
¼ cup (½ stick) butter or
   margarine, cut into chunks
Water
4 ounces American cheese slices

Combine the potatoes, seasoned salt and pepper in a bowl and mix well. Spoon into a baking dish. Top with the butter and a few tablespoons of water. Bake, covered with foil, at 350 degrees for 45 minutes. Remove the foil. Cover the potatoes with the cheese slices. Bake for 5 to 10 minutes longer or until the cheese melts.

Yield: 6 servings

80

Potato Sticks

$^1/_4$ *cup flour*
$^1/_2$ *teaspoon salt*
$1^1/_2$ *cups milk*
1 (10-ounce) can cream of celery
    soup
8 ounces American cheese, cubed
5 to 6 baking potatoes, peeled and
    cut as for French fries
1 cup chopped onion
Paprika

Combine the flour and salt in a saucepan. Whisk in the milk until smooth. Bring to a boil. Cook for 2 minutes, stirring constantly. Remove from the heat. Whisk in the soup and cheese. Combine the potatoes and onion in a greased 9×13-inch baking dish. Top with the cheese sauce. Bake at 350 degrees for 55 to 60 minutes or until the potatoes are tender. Sprinkle with paprika before serving.

Yield: 6 servings

81

Rice—Make It Twice As Nice

Rice is an easy side dish that will complement just about any meal. If you would like to give your rice some extra flavor, try substituting chicken broth, beef broth, or beef consommé for the water. Want to add a citrus twist? Try apple juice or orange juice in place of the water. This fruit-flavored rice is a great accompaniment to chicken or pork.

Spinach, Leek and Rice Casserole

1 (10-ounce) package frozen
    chopped spinach
1 small to medium leek, split
    lengthwise and sliced
2 cups cooked brown rice or white
    rice
2 eggs, lightly beaten
1 (14-ounce) can evaporated milk
2 tablespoons butter or margarine
1 1/2 cups (6 ounces) shredded
    Cheddar cheese
Salt to taste

Cook the spinach using the package directions; drain. Squeeze to remove any excess liquid. Combine the spinach, leek, rice, eggs, evaporated milk, butter, cheese and salt in a bowl and mix well. Spoon into a greased 1 1/2-quart baking dish. Bake for 45 to 60 minutes or until a knife inserted in the center comes out clean.

Yield: 4 to 5 servings

Spinach Casserole

3 (10-ounce) packages frozen
    chopped spinach
2 cups sour cream
1 envelope onion soup mix
Shredded Cheddar cheese

Cook the spinach using the package directions; drain. Squeeze to remove any excess liquid. Combine the spinach, sour cream and soup mix in a bowl and stir well. Spread in a greased baking dish. Sprinkle with cheese. Bake at 350 degrees for 30 minutes or until bubbly.

Yield: 4 to 6 servings

Note: This casserole works well as an appetizer dip. Chill the dip and serve it spooned into a hollowed-out round loaf of pumpernickel.

Squash Casserole

2 pounds zucchini or summer
    squash, cubed, cooked and
    drained
1 cup sour cream
1 (10-ounce) can cream of
    chicken soup
1 medium onion, finely chopped
2 medium carrots, grated
White wine or chicken broth
1 (8-ounce) package herb stuffing
    mix (fine or cubed)
3/4 cup (1 1/2 sticks) butter or
    margarine, melted

Combine the squash, sour cream, soup, onion and carrots in a bowl and mix well. Add a little white wine or chicken broth to thin the mixture if necessary. Combine the stuffing mix and butter in a bowl and mix well. Layer 1/2 of the stuffing mixture in a 9×13-inch baking dish coated with nonstick cooking spray. Layer with the squash mixture and remaining stuffing mix. Bake at 350 degrees for 30 to 45 minutes or until brown and bubbly.

Yield: 8 to 12 servings

83

Grammy's Macaroni

16 ounces elbow macaroni, cooked
    just until tender and drained
Salt and pepper to taste
2 cups (8 ounces) shredded sharp
    white New York or Vermont
    Cheddar cheese
Milk
2 tablespoons butter
$1/2$ cup dried bread crumbs

Layer $1/3$ of the macaroni, salt, pepper and $1/2$ of the cheese in a greased 8×12-inch baking dish. Layer with $1/3$ of the remaining macaroni, salt, pepper, remaining cheese and remaining macaroni. Pour enough milk into the baking dish to just reach the top layer of the macaroni. Melt the butter in a small saucepan. Add the bread crumbs and mix well. Sprinkle over the macaroni. Bake at 375 degrees for 30 to 35 minutes or until light brown and bubbly.

Yield: 8 to 10 servings

84

Pineapple Casserole

1 (20-ounce) can pineapple chunks
1/2 cup sugar
3 tablespoons flour
1/2 cup (2 ounces) shredded sharp
   Cheddar cheese
1/4 cup (1/2 stick) butter or
   margarine, melted
1/2 cup crushed butter crackers

Drain the pineapple, reserving 3 tablespoons juice. Combine the reserved juice, sugar and flour in a large bowl and mix well. Stir in the cheese and pineapple. Spoon into a greased 1-quart baking dish. Combine the butter and cracker crumbs in a small bowl and mix well. Sprinkle over the pineapple mixture. Bake at 300 degrees for 20 to 30 minutes.

Yield: 6 servings

Note: This recipe may easily be doubled.

85

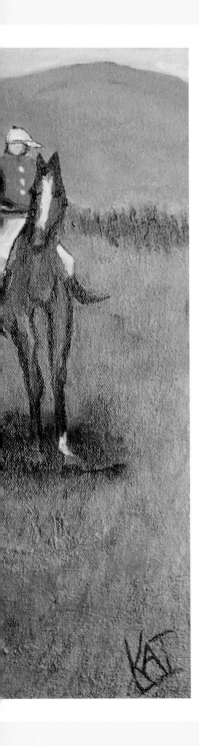

Bet the Main Event

And they're off! Ohio Valley locals and visitors have been "making tracks" to some exciting entertainment and off-track gambling venues reminiscent of Atlantic City since the early '50s. From greyhound racing at Wheeling Downs Racetrack and Gaming Center to thoroughbred racing at Mountaineer Racetrack and Gaming Resort, excitement runs wild on the banks of the Ohio River. Each has recently added video-slot machines, fine dining, and luxury accommodations that tempt anyone's entertainment palate. Live shows and the competitive excitement add flair to the Ohio Valley region. Main course entrées, both ordinary and extraordinary, always finish first.

Artist Kathryn Thalman loves horses, and her interpretation of "A Day at the Races," originally painted by Edgar Degas, is a true work of love. Ms. Thalman began drawing and painting almost before she could walk, crediting her grandfather Edward F. Stuntz and his "evening art lessons." By day, Ms. Thalman works in the world of corporate sales.

Working Person's Roast

1 (3- to 4-pound) beef roast or pork
   roast
1 (10-ounce) can cream of
   mushroom soup
1 envelope onion soup mix
2 tablespoons Worcestershire sauce
1 garlic clove
Seasoned salt to taste (optional)

Place the roast in a slow cooker. Combine the cream of mushroom soup, soup mix, Worcestershire sauce, garlic and seasoned salt in a bowl and mix well. Spoon over the roast. Cook on Low for 8 hours.

Yield: 6 servings

Note: This makes a great gravy.

Marinated Flank Steak

1 cup fat-free Italian dressing
1 cup dry red wine
1/3 cup green onions, sliced
3/4 cup soy sauce
1 lemon, thinly sliced
1 teaspoon dry mustard
1/2 teaspoon lemon pepper
2 garlic cloves, minced
2 (1- to 1 1/2-pound) flank steaks,
   scored

Combine the Italian dressing, wine, green onions, soy sauce, lemon, dry mustard, lemon pepper and garlic in a shallow glass dish or sealable plastic bag and mix well. Add the steaks. Marinate, covered, in the refrigerator for 8 hours or longer. Drain the steaks, discarding the marinade. Broil or grill over hot coals for 4 to 5 minutes on each side or to the desired degree of doneness. Cut the steak cross grain into thin slices. Serve as an entrée or as an appetizer on toast points with horseradish sauce or Dijon mustard.

Yield: 8 entrée or 24 appetizer servings

89

Flank Steak Marinade

1 small onion, chopped
$^1/_2$ cup red wine
2 tablespoons olive oil
1 tablespoon wine vinegar
1 garlic clove, crushed, or garlic
   powder to taste
$^1/_2$ teaspoon basil
$^1/_4$ teaspoon rosemary

Combine the onion, wine, olive oil, vinegar, garlic, basil and rosemary in a shallow glass dish and mix well. Use to marinate scored flank steak or London broil. Marinate, covered, in the refrigerator for 8 hours or longer. Cook as desired.

Yield: about 1 cup

The Tough Made Tender

A marinade is a great way to tenderize a tough cut of meat while boosting the flavor at the same time. To be effective, a marinade must have an acid in its ingredients to denature the proteins in the meat muscle. Besides leaving the meat to absorb the marinade from the outside, you can increase the tenderizing effect by injecting some of the marinade deep into the meat. Check your local kitchen supply store for the appropriate injector.

Oven Pepper Steak

1 (1¹/₂- to 2-pound) round steak,
    frozen then partially thawed
Meat tenderizer
Garlic powder
Flour
2 tablespoons vegetable oil
2 to 3 red bell peppers or green bell
    peppers, sliced
1 large onion, chopped or sliced
    into rings
2 large ribs celery, sliced
1 (28-ounce) can stewed tomatoes
1 (15-ounce) can tomato sauce
1 teaspoon salt
¹/₂ teaspoon pepper
Hot cooked rice or noodles

Pierce the steak all over with a fork and sprinkle with meat tenderizer and garlic powder. Cut into ¹/₂×2¹/₂-inch strips. Coat with flour. Brown in the oil in a skillet over high heat. Combine the browned steak, bell peppers, onion, celery, stewed tomatoes, tomato sauce, salt and pepper in a roasting pan and mix well. Bake, covered, at 325 degrees for 2 hours. Uncover and bake for 30 minutes longer. Serve over rice or noodles.

Yield: 6 to 8 servings

91

Meat Loaf

1¹/₂ pounds ground beef
1¹/₂ cups cooked rice or bread
   crumbs
2 eggs
1 (6-ounce) can tomato paste
¹/₂ envelope onion soup mix,
   combined with ¹/₄ cup water
¹/₂ green bell pepper, finely
   chopped
Salt and pepper to taste

Combine the ground beef, rice, eggs, ¹/₂ of the can of tomato paste, soup mix, bell pepper, salt and pepper in a bowl and mix well. Shape into a loaf in a baking dish. Bake at 350 degrees for 1¹/₄ hours. Top with the remaining tomato paste.

Yield: 4 to 6 servings

Cabbage Roll Casserole

2 pounds ground beef
3¹/₂ pounds cabbage, chopped
1 cup chopped onion
1 (28-ounce) can tomato sauce
1 cup uncooked rice
1 teaspoon salt
2 (14-ounce) cans beef broth

Brown the ground beef in a skillet, stirring until crumbly; drain. Combine the ground beef, cabbage, onions, tomato sauce, rice and salt in a bowl and mix well. Spread in a 9×13-inch baking dish. Pour the beef broth over the ground beef mixture. Bake, covered, at 350 degrees for 1¹/₂ hours, stirring once after the first hour.

Yield: 8 to 10 servings

92

Mexican Lasagna

1 pound ground beef
Cilantro (optional)
Cumin (optional)
Red pepper (optional)
1 (30-ounce) can chili beans
1 (10-ounce) can cream of
chicken soup
1 (10-ounce) can cream of
mushroom soup
1 (10-ounce) can enchilada sauce
1 (16-ounce) jar salsa
1 (2-ounce) can sliced black olives
8 or 9 flour tortillas
4 cups (16 ounces) shredded
Monterey Jack and Cheddar
cheese

Brown the ground beef with cilantro, cumin and red pepper in a skillet, stirring until the ground beef is crumbly; drain. Combine the chili beans, cream of chicken soup, cream of mushroom soup, enchilada sauce, salsa and black olives in a bowl and mix well. Layer the tortillas, browned ground beef, bean mixture and cheese $1/3$ at a time in a greased lasagna pan. Bake at 350 degrees for 30 to 40 minutes or until brown and bubbly.

Yield: 6 to 8 servings

Note: This dish works well with chicken instead of ground beef or without meat as a vegetarian entrée.

93

"White Castle" Hamburgers

1 pound ground beef
1 envelope onion soup mix
1 1/2 cups (6 ounces) shredded
   Cheddar cheese
2 tablespoons mayonnaise
8 hamburger buns
Dill pickle chips

Brown the ground beef in a skillet, stirring until crumbly; drain. Combine the browned ground beef, soup mix, cheese and mayonnaise in a bowl and mix well. Spread a portion of the ground beef mixture on the bottom of each hamburger bun. Top with 2 or 3 pickle chips. Replace the bun tops. Wrap the buns individually in foil. Arrange on a baking sheet. Bake at 325 degrees for 30 minutes.

Yield: 6 to 8 servings

Note: Assemble, wrap and chill the buns ahead of time if you wish. Bake them just before serving. They also freeze and reheat well. To reduce calories without giving up taste, substitute reduced-fat or fat-free cheese, mayonnaise and buns.

Sloppy Joes

1 pound ground beef
1 cup chopped onion
1 (15-ounce) can tomato sauce
1/2 cup ketchup
1/3 cup packed brown sugar
2 teaspoons prepared mustard
Cayenne pepper to taste (optional)
Hamburger buns

Brown the ground beef and onion in a skillet, stirring until the ground beef is crumbly; drain. Combine the tomato sauce, ketchup, brown sugar, mustard and cayenne pepper in a saucepan and mix well. Stir in the ground beef mixture. Bring to a boil. Reduce the heat and simmer for 15 to 20 minutes. Serve over hamburger buns.

Yield: 4 servings

Skillet Sausage and Potatoes

3 to 4 tablespoons olive oil
1 3/4 pounds red potatoes, cubed
2 medium onions, chopped
8 ounces sausage, sliced 1/4 inch
    thick
2 tablespoons chopped fresh thyme,
    or 1 teaspoon dried
1 1/2 teaspoons cumin
1/4 teaspoon salt
1/4 teaspoon pepper

Heat the olive oil in a skillet over medium heat. Add the potatoes and onions. Cook for 12 minutes, stirring frequently. Add the sausage. Cook for 10 minutes, stirring frequently. Stir in the thyme, cumin, salt and pepper. Cook for 1 to 2 minutes longer.

Yield: 4 to 6 servings

95

Citrus-Marinated Pork Chops

Juice of 2 limes
Juice of 2 oranges
1 1/2 tablespoons balsamic vinegar
1 tablespoon olive oil
1 tablespoon Dijon mustard
2 to 3 garlic cloves, minced
2 to 3 sprigs of rosemary or thyme,
  or 1/2 teaspoon dried rosemary
  or thyme
1/2 teaspoon salt
1/2 teaspoon pepper
4 boneless pork chops
1 teaspoon olive oil
1 tablespoon butter

Combine the lime juice, orange juice, vinegar, 1 tablespoon olive oil, Dijon mustard, garlic, rosemary, salt and pepper in a shallow glass dish and mix well. Add the pork chops. Marinate, covered, in the refrigerator for at least 30 minutes. Drain the chops, reserving the marinade. Sauté the chops in 1 teaspoon olive oil in a skillet for 5 minutes on each side. Add the marinade. Bring to a boil. Reduce the heat and simmer, covered, for 7 minutes or until the chops are cooked through, turning once. Remove the chops to a serving dish. Bring the liquid in the skillet to a boil. Cook, stirring, until the liquid has reduced to a thick sauce. Stir in the butter. Strain the sauce and pour over the chops.

Yield: 4 servings

96

Ham Loaf

*2 pounds canned processed ham
    loaf, crumbled*
2 eggs
1 can bread crumbs
¹/₂ cup tomato soup
¹/₂ cup evaporated milk
¹/₃ cup ketchup
3 tablespoons prepared mustard
2 tablespoons cider vinegar
¹/₂ cup packed brown sugar

Combine the crumbled ham loaf, eggs, bread crumbs, tomato soup and evaporated milk in a bowl and mix well. Lightly pack the mixture into a greased loaf pan. Bake, covered with foil, at 350 degrees for 1 hour. Pour off the drippings. Combine the ketchup, prepared mustard, vinegar and brown sugar in a small bowl. Spread a small amount over the ham loaf. Bake, uncovered, for 30 minutes longer. Serve with the remaining ketchup mixture.

Yield: 6 to 8 servings

Note: This dish is one of Brad Paisley's favorites, as prepared by his mother.

97

Chicken Roll-Ups

2 cups chopped cooked chicken
1 cup (4 ounces) shredded Cheddar
   cheese
1 (8-count) can crescent rolls
1 (10-ounce) can cream of
   chicken soup
Milk
1 (2-ounce) jar pimentos (optional)

Combine the chicken and cheese in a bowl and mix well. Unroll the crescent roll dough and separate into triangles. Spread with the chicken mixture. Roll up from the wide ends. Place the rolls in a baking dish. Combine the cream of chicken soup, 1 soup can of milk and pimentos in a bowl and mix well. Pour over the crescent rolls. Bake at 350 degrees for 30 minutes or until brown. Serve with rice.

Yield: 6 to 8 servings

Roasted Chicken

1 (3-pound) chicken
2 lemons, pierced
1 tablespoon kosher salt
1 teaspoon minced garlic
1 cup water

Rinse the chicken and pat dry. Place the lemons inside the chicken cavity. Combine the kosher salt and garlic in a bowl and mix well. Rub over the outside of the chicken. Place the chicken on a rack in a roasting pan and pour the water into the bottom of the pan. Roast at 400 degrees for 1 hour or until cooked through.

Yield: 4 to 6 servings

Rosemary Chicken

3/4 cup chardonnay
1/3 cup olive oil
6 garlic cloves
Juice of 1/2 lemon
1 tablespoon fresh rosemary
1 teaspoon salt
Pepper to taste
2 1/2 to 3 pounds chicken pieces

Combine the chardonnay, olive oil, garlic, lemon juice, rosemary, salt and pepper in a blender and process until smooth. Pour over the chicken in a baking dish and let marinate for 30 minutes. Bake at 375 degrees for 50 to 60 minutes or until cooked through.

Yield: 6 to 8 servings

Teriyaki Marinade for Chicken or Steak

3/4 cup vegetable oil
1/4 cup soy sauce
1/4 cup honey
2 tablespoons white vinegar
3 green onions, chopped
1 garlic clove, minced
1 1/2 teaspoons ginger

Combine the oil, soy sauce, honey, vinegar, green onions, garlic and ginger in a shallow glass dish and mix well. Use to marinate chicken or flank steak. Marinate, covered, in the refrigerator for at least 4 hours, turning occasionally. Cook as desired.

Yield: about 1 1/4 cups

99

Chicken with Garlic and Mushrooms

2 eggs
1 teaspoon garlic powder
Salt and pepper to taste
1 cup Italian bread crumbs
$1/2$ cup (2 ounces) grated Parmesan
   cheese
$1/2$ teaspoon garlic powder
6 boneless skinless chicken breasts
1 cup (2 sticks) butter
1 teaspoon finely chopped fresh
   parsley
Juice of $1/2$ lemon
$1/2$ teaspoon garlic powder
8 ounces mushrooms, sliced

Whisk the eggs, 1 teaspoon garlic powder, salt and pepper in a shallow bowl. Mix the bread crumbs, cheese and $1/2$ teaspoon garlic powder on a plate. Dip the chicken in the egg mixture and then coat with the bread crumb mixture. Place in a greased baking dish. Melt the butter in a small saucepan. Add the parsley, lemon juice and $1/2$ teaspoon garlic powder and mix well. Pour $1/2$ of the butter mixture over the chicken. Bake at 375 degrees for 25 to 30 minutes or until the chicken is cooked through. Top with the mushrooms and the remaining butter mixture. Bake for 5 to 10 minutes longer.

Yield: 6 servings

100

Crispy Dijon Chicken

1/4 cup plain yogurt
1/2 teaspoon salt-free herb
   seasoning blend
1/2 teaspoon lemon juice
1/2 teaspoon Dijon mustard
1/2 cup cornflakes, crushed
1/4 cup (1 ounce) grated Parmesan
   cheese
2 to 4 boneless skinless chicken
   breasts

Whisk the yogurt, herb seasoning, lemon juice and Dijon mustard in a shallow bowl. Mix the cornflake crumbs and cheese on a plate. Dip the chicken in the yogurt mixture and then coat with the cornflake mixture. Place in a greased baking dish. Bake at 350 degrees for 35 to 45 minutes or until cooked through.

Yield: 2 to 4 servings

Grammy's Chicken Supreme

4 cups chopped cooked chicken
1 (10-ounce) can cream of
   mushroom soup
1 (8-ounce) can sliced water
   chestnuts, drained
1 1/2 cups diced celery
1 cup mayonnaise
1/2 package corn bread or herb
   stuffing mix
1/2 cup (1 stick) butter, melted

Combine the chicken, cream of mushroom soup, water chestnuts, celery and mayonnaise in a bowl and mix well. Spoon into a greased baking dish. Combine the stuffing mix and butter in a bowl and mix well. Sprinkle over the chicken mixture. Bake at 350 degrees for 40 to 45 minutes or until golden brown.

Yield: 4 to 6 servings

101

Chicken Jambalaya

¹⁄₃ *cup chopped celery*
¹⁄₄ cup chopped onion
¹⁄₄ cup chopped green bell pepper
2 tablespoons butter or margarine
1 (14-ounce) can diced tomatoes
1¹⁄₂ cups chicken broth
²⁄₃ cup rice
1 teaspoon basil
¹⁄₂ teaspoon garlic salt
¹⁄₄ teaspoon pepper
Hot red pepper sauce to taste
1 bay leaf
2 cups chopped cooked chicken

Cook the celery, onion and bell pepper in the butter in a large skillet or saucepan until the vegetables are tender, stirring frequently. Add the diced tomatoes, chicken broth, rice, basil, garlic salt, pepper, hot red pepper sauce and bay leaf and mix well. Bring to a boil. Reduce the heat and simmer, covered, for 20 minutes or until the rice is tender, stirring frequently. Stir in the chicken. Cook until heated through. Discard the bay leaf.

Yield: 4 servings

Note: This is a great make-ahead dish.

102

Slow Cooker Peppers Stuffed with Couscous and Turkey

4 large red bell peppers or green
*   bell peppers*
1/2 pound ground turkey or beef
1/2 cup chopped onion
1 garlic clove, minced
1 (15-ounce) can tomato sauce
1/2 teaspoon cumin
1/4 teaspoon cinnamon
1/4 teaspoon salt
1/8 teaspoon red pepper
2/3 cup uncooked couscous
1/2 cup water or vegetable juice
Pine nuts (optional)

Cut off the tops of the bell peppers. Remove the membranes and seeds. Rinse the bell peppers. Brown the ground turkey, onion and garlic in a skillet, stirring until the turkey is crumbly; drain. Add the tomato sauce, cumin, cinnamon, salt, red pepper and couscous and mix well. Fill each bell pepper with 1/4 of the turkey mixture. Pour the water into a slow cooker. Stand the bell peppers upright in the cooker. Cook on Low for 5 to 7 hours or until the bell peppers are tender. Sprinkle with pine nuts.

Yield: 4 servings

Note: If you double the recipe, you may not want to double the cinnamon. Taste the filling before you increase the amount.

103

From Creeks to Rivers

The "River City" of Wheeling brings many images to mind. The river and its tributaries are what brought prosperity and industry to a new land. The Suspension Bridge, constructed in the 1830s, was a gateway to the west that remains standing today. It is lighted every night, showing its span across the great Ohio River.

The new Heritage Port invites any and all to sit and watch water enthusiasts and is home to some local events and a community-built playground that incorporates water and land as one.

A mainstay in Northern West Virginia's history and growth, water brings to mind some good seafood and dishes from some of America's most famous waterways. Coleman's Fish Market of Wheeling is famous for its Whitefish Sandwich and selection of fresh seafood. The frequent long lines are testimony to that.

Local residents share their own "treasures from the deep" with a flair, rivaling some of the greatest harbor towns and seashores, from our waterways to yours.

"Oglebay Falls Drive" by Lenora Turbanic in an oil medium. Self-taught in the art of watercolors following some experience in oils, Mrs. Turbanic prefers the "cleaner" medium with water. Her first attempts became greeting cards for friends and family, and her subjects are mostly animals.

Eleanor Weaver

Shirley Weaver

Mary (Weaver) Renner

Beth Weaver

Crab Cakes with Lime Sauce

²/₃ cup mayonnaise
1 tablespoon lime juice
¹/₄ teaspoon cayenne pepper
1 (16-ounce) can lump crab meat,
   drained and flaked
¹/₂ cup bread crumbs
2 (2-ounce) jars pimentos
2 tablespoons minced green onions
¹/₂ cup bread crumbs
Butter
Lime Sauce

Combine the mayonnaise, lime juice and cayenne pepper in a bowl and mix well. Stir in the crab meat, ¹/₂ cup bread crumbs, pimentos and green onions. Shape into 8 patties and coat them with ¹/₂ cup bread crumbs. Sauté the crab cakes in butter in a skillet for 3 minutes on each side, turning carefully. Serve with the Lime Sauce on the side.

Yield: 8 servings

Note: These crab cakes may be baked instead of fried. You may also substitute olive oil for the butter.

LIME SAUCE

¹/₂ cup mayonnaise
¹/₄ cup sour cream
1 tablespoon lime juice
2 teaspoons lime zest

Combine the mayonnaise, sour cream, lime juice and lime zest in a bowl and mix well.

107

Crab Spread on English Muffins

1 (5-ounce) jar Old English cheese
  spread
1/2 cup (1 stick) butter, softened
2 tablespoons mayonnaise
1 (6-ounce) can lump crab meat,
  drained and flaked
1/2 teaspoon garlic salt
1/2 teaspoon seasoned salt
1 package English muffins

Beat the cheese spread, butter and mayonnaise in a bowl. Add the crab meat, garlic salt and seasoned salt and mix well. Spread on the English muffin halves. Cut the halves into quarters. Arrange on a baking sheet. Broil for 5 to 10 minutes or until golden brown.

Yield: 48 appetizer servings

New Orleans Crab Dip

4 ounces fat-free cream cheese,
  softened
1/2 cup fat-free mayonnaise
1 (8-ounce) package imitation crab
  meat, chopped
1/4 cup chopped celery
1/4 cup chopped green bell pepper
1 garlic clove, pressed
1 to 11/2 teaspoons Cajun
  seasoning

Beat the cream cheese and mayonnaise in a bowl. Add the crab meat, celery, bell pepper, garlic and Cajun seasoning and mix well. Remove to a chilled bowl. Serve with toast or crackers.

Yield: 12 servings

108

Creamy Crab and Artichoke Dip

8 ounces cream cheese, softened
1 cup mayonnaise
8 ounces crab meat
1/3 cup chopped onion
1 (14-ounce) can artichoke hearts,
*   drained and chopped*
3/4 cup (3 ounces) grated Parmesan
*   cheese*

Beat the cream cheese and mayonnaise in a bowl. Add the crab meat, onion, artichoke hearts and cheese and mix well. Spread in a glass pie plate. Bake at 375 degrees for 15 to 18 minutes or until heated through and light brown. Serve with butter crackers.

Yield: 15 to 20 servings

Hot Crab Dip

1 cup crab meat
8 ounces cream cheese, softened
1 tablespoon milk
2 tablespoons chopped onion
1/2 teaspoon horseradish
Salt and pepper to taste
2 ounces slivered almonds

Combine the crab meat, cream cheese, milk, onion, horseradish, salt and pepper in a bowl and mix well. Spread in a baking dish. Top with the almonds. Bake at 350 degrees for 20 minutes.

Yield: 10 to 12 servings

109

Shrimp Butter

2 (4-ounce) cans small shrimp, or 8
    ounces peeled cooked shrimp
8 ounces cream cheese, softened
$^1/_2$ cup (1 stick) butter, softened
$^1/_4$ cup mayonnaise
1 to 2 tablespoons grated onion
2 tablespoons lemon juice

Chop the shrimp in a food processor by pulsing 4 or 5 times. Beat the cream cheese, butter and mayonnaise in a bowl. Add the shrimp, onion and lemon juice and mix well. Chill for several hours or overnight.

Yield: 10 to 12 servings

Shrimp Gelatin Mold

$1^1/_2$ envelopes unflavored gelatin
$^1/_2$ cup cold water
1 (10-ounce) can tomato soup
8 ounces cream cheese, softened
1 cup mayonnaise
$^1/_4$ cup diced onion
1 pound peeled cooked shrimp,
    chopped
$1^1/_2$ cups diced celery

Soften the gelatin in the cold water and stir until dissolved. Combine the dissolved gelatin, tomato soup, cream cheese, mayonnaise and onion in a mixing bowl and blend until smooth. Add the shrimp and celery and mix well. Spoon into an oiled decorative mold. Chill until set. Unmold onto a serving plate.

Yield: 8 to 10 servings

110

Creole Shrimp and Chicken

1 pound medium shrimp, peeled
    and deveined
1 teaspoon salt
4 boneless skinless chicken breasts
3 tablespoons vegetable oil
1/2 cup diced green bell pepper
1 small onion, diced
1 (10-ounce) can diced tomatoes
1/2 cup dry sherry
1 tablespoon Worcestershire sauce
1/4 teaspoon thyme
2 tablespoons chopped fresh
    parsley
1 1/2 teaspoons salt
1/2 teaspoon pepper
1 cup half-and-half
Hot cooked long grain and wild rice

ring the shrimp, water to cover and 1 teaspoon salt to a boil in a saucepan. Boil for 2 to 3 minutes or until the shrimp turn pink. Drain and chill. Brown the chicken in the oil in a skillet. Let cool and cut into bite-size pieces. Add the bell pepper and onion to the remaining oil in the skillet. Sauté for 4 to 5 minutes or until tender. Add the tomatoes, sherry, Worcestershire sauce, thyme, parsley, salt and pepper. Add the chicken and mix well. Pour into a greased 4-quart casserole. Bake at 350 degrees for 45 minutes. Stir the shrimp and half-and-half into the chicken mixture. Return to the oven and cook until heated through. Serve over long grain and wild rice.

Yield: 6 servings

111

Orange Ginger Shrimp Skewers

1/2 cup fresh orange juice
2 tablespoons minced green onions
1 tablespoon ginger
1 teaspoon chopped fresh cilantro
2 tablespoons rice vinegar
2 tablespoons soy sauce
1 tablespoon vegetable oil
2 teaspoons grated orange peel
*1 pound large shrimp, peeled and
    deveined*
*2 oranges, peeled, sectioned and
    halved*

Combine the orange juice, green onions, ginger, cilantro, vinegar, soy sauce, oil and orange peel in a large bowl and mix well. Add the shrimp and toss to coat. Marinate, covered, in the refrigerator for 15 minutes. Remove the shrimp from the marinade, reserving marinade. Thread the shrimp and oranges alternately onto each of 8 skewers. Grill for 4 minutes per side or until shrimp are opaque, basting with the reserved marinade.

Yield: 8 servings

112

Spicy Jumbo Shrimp

1 pound jumbo shrimp, peeled and
    deveined
1 teaspoon extra-virgin olive oil
$^1/_2$ cup white wine, or $^1/_2$ cup water
    mixed with 3 tablespoons lemon
    juice
1 hot chile pepper, chopped (wear
    gloves when handling)
1 tablespoon lemon juice
Dash of hot red pepper sauce

Sauté the shrimp in the olive oil in a nonstick skillet for 1 minute. Add the wine, chile pepper, lemon juice and hot red pepper sauce. Cook, covered, for 3 minutes or until the shrimp turn pink. Remove the shrimp to a serving bowl. Cook the sauce over high heat for 3 minutes. Pour over the shrimp. Serve warm or cold.

Yield: 4 servings

Spaghetti and Scallops

1 pound bay scallops
$^1/_2$ to 1 teaspoon minced garlic
2 tablespoons butter or margarine
1 (16-ounce) package frozen
    broccoli, carrots and cauliflower
    mixture, cooked
2 tablespoons butter or margarine
Freshly grated Parmesan cheese
16 ounces spaghetti, fettuccini or
    angel hair pasta, cooked and
    drained

Sauté the scallops and garlic in 2 tablespoons butter in a skillet until the scallops are tender. Sauté the cooked vegetables in 2 tablespoons butter in another skillet until heated through. Add the scallops and stir well. Sprinkle with cheese. Serve over the spaghetti.

Yield: 2 to 4 servings

113

Salmon Patties

1 (6-ounce) can boneless salmon,
    drained
³/₄ cup crushed saltines or ³/₄ cup
    plain or Italian bread crumbs
¹/₂ medium onion, minced
¹/₄ teaspoon salt
¹/₄ teaspoon pepper
1 egg, beaten
2 tablespoons mayonnaise
Juice of ¹/₂ lemon
    (about 1 tablespoon)
Dashes of Worcestershire sauce
Bread crumbs
2 tablespoons butter
2 tablespoons vegetable oil

Combine the salmon, saltines, onion, salt and pepper in a bowl and mix well. Whisk the egg, mayonnaise, lemon juice and Worcestershire sauce in a bowl. Add to the salmon mixture and mix well. Shape into appetizer-size patties or larger entrée-size patties. Coat with bread crumbs. Sauté in the butter and oil in a skillet until golden brown on both sides.

Yield: 4 to 8 servings

Note: For more flavor, add ¹/₄ cup finely chopped green onions and/or ¹/₄ cup minced red bell pepper.

114

Marinated Grilled Fillet of Salmon

4 salmon fillets
Blackened seasoning to taste
Pepper to taste
1/4 cup olive oil
6 ounces Jack Daniel's whiskey
1/4 cup packed brown sugar
4 pats of seasoned butter

Sprinkle the fillets with blackened seasoning and pepper. Place the fillets in a shallow glass dish. Combine the olive oil, whiskey and brown sugar in a bowl and mix well. Pour over the fillets. Marinate, covered, in the refrigerator for 2 to 3 hours. Discard the marinade. Grill the fillets skin side up on a rack over medium-hot coals for 3 minutes. Rotate the fillets to create angled grill marks. Grill for 2 minutes. Turn over the fillets carefully. Cover the grill to trap smoke and grill for 4 to 5 minutes or until the fillets flake easily. Top each fillet with a pat of seasoned butter. Garnish with lemon slices and sprigs of fresh dillweed.

Yield: 4 servings

Note: This is another of Brad Paisley's favorite dishes, as prepared by his mother.

115

Our Own Brad Paisley

It's impossible to talk about the Ohio Valley without mentioning Brad Paisley, a noted country music star born and raised in our very own backyard. Paisley's music career began at the age of eight, when his grandfather gave him his first guitar. His first song, "Born on Christmas Day," was written when he was only twelve. At age fourteen, Brad started playing at the Jamboree in the Hills, and by twenty, he was already in Nashville showing everyone what he was all about. The Glen Dale native was inducted into the Grand Ole Opry in February 2001 at the ripe age of twenty-eight. It is obvious to all who love country music that we haven't seen or heard the last of Brad, as down our river, a star was born.

Lemon Caper Tuna Spread

1 (3-ounce) can solid water-packed
* tuna, drained*
2 tablespoons nonfat cream cheese,
* softened*
1 tablespoon nonfat mayonnaise
1 tablespoon lemon juice
2 tablespoons chopped fresh
* parsley*
1 teaspoon chopped fresh marjoram
2 dashes of hot red pepper sauce
2 tablespoons drained capers

Combine the tuna, cream cheese, mayonnaise, lemon juice, parsley, marjoram and hot red pepper sauce in a food processor and process until smooth. Remove to a small serving bowl. Stir in the capers. Serve as a sandwich filling with sliced tomatoes and lettuce.

Yield: 4 to 6 servings

Note: This spread makes a delicious filling for cherry tomatoes.

116

Fantastically Simple Baked Fish Fillets

2 pounds fish fillets
1 cup sour cream
3 tablespoons minced onion
1 tablespoon parsley flakes
1 teaspoon seasoned salt
1 teaspoon paprika
Butter

Place the fillets in a single layer in a buttered baking dish. Combine the sour cream, onion and parsley in a bowl. Spoon over the fillets. Sprinkle with the seasoned salt and paprika. Dot with butter. Bake at 400 degrees for 15 to 25 minutes or until the fillets flake easily.

Yield: 4 servings

117

Ciao, Baby

The Italian heritage is more than an influence in the
Ohio Valley; it's a way of life.

From Wheeling's Italian Festival each summer to our
fine family-owned Italian restaurants, any visitor or
resident can enjoy authentic cuisine right here in our
own backyard. The owners welcome you into their
"homes" and engage you in true Italian conversation
and delicacies.

If you aren't Italian by descent, the Italian community
here has a flair for making you feel like you are.
We celebrate their fine heritage and food. SALUT!

Accomplished photographer Cheryl Joseph presents "Little Chef." Her talent for capturing breathtaking scenery and the essence of people is very evident in her work. Recently, she has completed a personal genealogy study that took her and her talents to Italy, where she was united with distant relatives. She has a true love of Italy and its people, and that is reflected in her current gallery of photographs.

Glazed Meatballs

1 pound ground beef
1/2 cup bread crumbs
1/3 cup chopped onion
1 egg
1/4 cup milk
1 tablespoon parsley
1/2 teaspoon Worcestershire sauce
1 teaspoon salt
1/8 teaspoon pepper
1 (12-ounce) jar chili sauce
1 (10-ounce) jar grape jelly

Combine the ground beef, bread crumbs, onion, egg, milk, parsley, Worcestershire sauce, salt and pepper in a bowl and mix well. Shape into 1-inch meatballs. Brown the meatballs in a skillet; drain. Heat the chili sauce and jelly in a small saucepan until the jelly melts, stirring constantly. Add to the meatballs in the skillet. Simmer for 30 minutes, stirring occasionally. Serve hot.

Yield: 8 servings

Parmesan Potatoes

8 butter crackers, crumbled
1/4 cup (1 ounce) freshly grated
   Parmesan cheese
1 teaspoon garlic powder
1/2 teaspoon salt, or to taste
1/2 teaspoon pepper
1/2 teaspoon paprika
1 pound russet potatoes,
   cut into 1-inch cubes
1/4 cup (1/2 stick) butter, melted
1 tablespoon freshly grated
   Parmesan cheese

Combine the crackers, 1/4 cup cheese, garlic powder, salt, pepper and paprika in a sealable plastic bag. Shake well. Combine the potatoes and the melted butter in a bowl and stir to coat well. Remove the potatoes, reserving any leftover butter. Add the potatoes to the cracker mixture in batches. Shake to coat evenly. Arrange the potatoes in a single layer in a microwave-safe dish. Microwave, tightly covered, on High for 5 minutes. Add the reserved butter and stir well. Microwave on High for 2 to 3 minutes or until fork-tender. Sprinkle with 1 tablespoon cheese. Serve with wooden picks if desired.

Yield: 4 servings

121

Pesto Torte

Cream cheese, softened
Butter, softened
Chopped sun-dried tomatoes
Prepared traditional pesto
Prepared sun-dried tomato pesto

Combine equal portions of cream cheese and butter in a mixing bowl. Beat until smooth and creamy. Line a bowl with plastic wrap. Spray with nonstick cooking spray. Sprinkle the sun-dried tomatoes in the bottom of the bowl. Layer with the cream cheese mixture, traditional pesto, cream cheese mixture and sun-dried tomato pesto. Chill or freeze, covered, until serving time. Invert onto a serving platter.

Yield: variable

Chicken Tortellini Salad

1 medium chicken breast, cooked,
*   boned and shredded*
1 package frozen cheese tortellini,
*   cooked*
1 green bell pepper, cut into thin
*   strips*
1 red bell pepper, cut into thin strips
1 yellow bell pepper, cut into thin
*   strips*
2 carrots, shaved into wide strips
*   with a vegetable peeler*
1 pint grape tomatoes, halved
Ken's Steakhouse Caesar salad
*   dressing to taste*

Combine the shredded chicken, tortellini, bell peppers, carrots and tomatoes in a salad bowl. Add Caesar salad dressing and toss to mix.

Yield: 20 servings

Note: This salad is a great addition to a picnic or potluck dinner.

122

Winter Minestrone

1 large onion, finely chopped
1 rib celery, finely chopped
2 garlic cloves, minced
1 teaspoon basil
$1/2$ teaspoon rosemary
$1/2$ teaspoon oregano
$1/2$ teaspoon thyme
2 tablespoons olive oil
$1/4$ cup pearl barley
2 large potatoes, diced
3 large carrots, diced
8 cups low-sodium low-fat chicken
    broth
1 (15-ounce) can cannellini beans,
    drained and rinsed
$2/3$ cup small shell pasta
$1/4$ cup tomato paste
2 cups finely shredded cabbage
Grated Parmesan cheese to taste

Sauté the onion, celery, garlic, basil, rosemary, oregano and thyme in the olive oil in a soup pot for 5 minutes or until the onion is tender. Add the barley, potatoes, carrots and chicken broth. Bring to a boil. Reduce the heat and simmer, covered, for 20 to 30 minutes. Stir in the cannellini beans, pasta and tomato paste. Simmer until the pasta is al dente. Add the cabbage. Cook for 5 minutes longer or until the cabbage is tender-crisp. Serve with grated Parmesan cheese.

Yield: 4 servings

123

Pepper Pasta

1/2 pound boneless skinless chicken
    breasts
1/4 cup olive oil
1 cup quartered mushrooms
1/2 cup each sliced green, red and
    yellow bell peppers
1/2 medium red onion, sliced
6 to 8 plum tomatoes, sliced
2 teaspoons chopped garlic
1/2 cup white wine
1 1/2 cups tomato sauce
1/4 teaspoon crushed red pepper
Salt and black pepper to taste
16 ounces penne, cooked and
    drained
2 tablespoons chopped fresh basil
2 tablespoons grated Parmesan
    cheese

Cut the chicken into bite-size pieces if desired. Cook the chicken in the olive oil in a large saucepan over medium-high heat for 5 to 7 minutes, turning frequently. Add the mushrooms, bell peppers, onion, tomatoes and garlic. Sauté until the vegetables are tender. Add the wine, tomato sauce and red pepper. Simmer for 15 to 20 minutes longer. Season with salt and black pepper. Serve over the cooked penne. Sprinkle with the basil and cheese.

Yield: 4 servings

124

Chicken Piccata

1 egg
1 tablespoon lemon juice
$^1/_4$ cup flour
Garlic powder to taste
Paprika to taste
4 boneless skinless chicken breasts
$^1/_4$ cup ($^1/_2$ stick) margarine
2 chicken bouillon cubes, dissolved
    in $^1/_2$ cup boiling water
2 tablespoons lemon juice

Whisk the egg and 1 tablespoon lemon juice in a shallow bowl. Mix the flour, garlic powder and paprika on a plate. Dip the chicken in the egg mixture, then in the flour mixture. Heat the margarine in a skillet. Brown the chicken on both sides in the margarine until cooked through. Add the bouillon and 2 tablespoons lemon juice to the skillet. Simmer, covered, for 20 minutes.

Yield: 4 servings

How to Select Your Wines

1. Follow the general rule "white with light and red with rich." The preparation of a dish—whether it has a light or a rich sauce, for example—is more important than what is being cooked. Game is a notable exception, however. Its richness calls for a red wine.

2. The acid of vinegar cuts the unctuousness of oil and vice versa. Apply this to wine and you see why acidic wines like pinot noir pair well with oily foods. This important principle is rarely touted by others.

3. While opposites balance, such as pairing a lightly sweet white (an Auslese, chenin blanc, etc.) with very spicy foods, never underestimate pairing similar flavors. Pinot noir stands up quite well to lemon, for example, no doubt because the high acids in each are complementary.

4. Match flavors. This principle is so simple that it is often overlooked. The grapefruit/citrus taste of sauvignon blanc goes as well with fish as lemon does, and for the same reason.

5. Avoid pairing foods with wines that are dominated by nonfood flavors. Oak is not a taste you expect to find in food. Therefore, save wines aged in oak for fireside chats and other nonfood events.

6. A slightly sweet wine, such as a California gewürztraminer, a German Spätlese, or an Anjou from France's Loire Valley, is sure to be a crowd pleaser when served with the right food.

7. Never pair a wine with any food that is sweeter than the wine. This makes the term "dessert wine" a misnomer. Most sweet wines are best enjoyed after dessert, though some swear by a combination of chocolate and cabernet sauvignon. Try a black muscat like Quady's Elysium.

8. Drink wine to enjoy it and the company with which you are sharing it. Food and wine pairings are elusive and to some degree mythical. Drink wine you like with food you like, but never stop experimenting.

125

Angel Hair with Chicken Casserole

1 large onion, finely chopped
1/2 cup (1 stick) butter, melted
4 cups chopped cooked chicken
2 (10-ounce) cans cream of
    chicken soup
2 cups sour cream
8 ounces angel hair pasta, cooked
    and drained
Seasoned salt
8 ounces Parmesan cheese, grated

Sauté the onion in the butter in a skillet until the onion is tender. Add the chicken, cream of chicken soup and sour cream and mix well. Stir in the pasta. Spoon the mixture into a 9×13-inch baking dish coated with nonstick cooking spray. Sprinkle with seasoned salt and the cheese. Bake at 350 degrees for 55 to 60 minutes or until light brown.

Yield: 6 to 8 servings

Note: Try this casserole with a thicker noodle if desired.

Slow Cooker Chicken Fettuccini

6 boneless skinless chicken breasts
2 tablespoons olive oil
1 (14-ounce) can diced tomatoes
1/4 cup chopped green onions
1 garlic clove, minced
1 tablespoon basil
1 teaspoon salt
1/2 cup heavy cream
2 egg yolks
*1/2 cup (2 ounces) grated Parmesan
   cheese*
*8 ounces fettuccini, cooked and
   drained*

Brown the chicken in the olive oil in a skillet. Remove to a slow cooker. Add the tomatoes, green onions, garlic, basil and salt. Cook on Low for 5 hours. Remove the chicken and cut into bite-size pieces. Return the chicken to the cooker. Stir in the cream, egg yolks and cheese. Cook on High for 30 minutes or until thickened. Add the fettuccini. Cook on High for 50 to 60 minutes.

Yield: 6 servings

Note: For a more generous amount of sauce with this dish, double the amount of cream, egg yolks and cheese.

127

Tuscan Roasted Game Hens

1 onion, diced
3 ribs celery, diced
2 large carrots, diced
6 Cornish game hens
2 teaspoons olive oil
3 garlic cloves, minced
2 teaspoons minced fresh rosemary
2 teaspoons minced fresh sage
2 teaspoons kosher salt
1 teaspoon cracked pepper
6 thin slices pancetta

Scatter the onion, celery and carrots in a roasting pan. Place the hens on top of the vegetables. Drizzle with the olive oil. Combine the garlic, rosemary, sage, kosher salt and pepper in a bowl. Rub the garlic mixture over the hens until well coated. Lay a slice of pancetta over the breast of each hen and secure with wooden picks. Roast at 425 degrees for 15 minutes. Reduce the oven temperature to 350 degrees. Roast for 45 minutes longer or until cooked through. Let the hens rest at room temperature for a few minutes before serving.

Yield: 6 servings

Note: Pancetta is an Italian ham—much like bacon. Prosciutto may be substituted.

Rigatoni with Four Cheeses

16 ounces rigatoni
3¹/₂ tablespoons unsalted butter,
    melted
1 cup heavy cream
¹/₂ cup (2 ounces) shredded Swiss
    cheese
¹/₂ cup (2 ounces) shredded fontina
    cheese
¹/₂ cup (2 ounces) shredded
    mozzarella cheese
¹/₂ cup (2 ounces) grated Parmesan
    cheese
Pinch of nutmeg

Cook the pasta in boiling salted water in a large saucepan for 8 minutes or until still firm; drain. Mix the pasta and butter in a large bowl. Stir in the cream, Swiss cheese, fontina cheese, mozzarella cheese and Parmesan cheese. Pour the pasta mixture into a buttered 3-quart casserole. Sprinkle with additional Parmesan cheese and nutmeg. Bake at 375 degrees for 15 to 20 minutes or until golden brown.

Yield: 6 servings

129

Penne with Sicilian Tomato Sauce

¹/₄ cup (1 ounce) grated Parmesan
  cheese
2 garlic cloves
2 cups loosely packed chopped
  fresh basil
¹/₄ cup olive oil
1¹/₂ pounds tomatoes, peeled,
  seeded and cut into chunks
¹/₂ teaspoon salt
¹/₈ teaspoon pepper
16 ounces penne or mostaccioli,
  cooked and drained

Combine the cheese and garlic in a food processor and pulse until the garlic is chopped. Add ¹/₂ of the basil and all of the olive oil. Process until the basil is chopped, scraping the sides. Add the remaining basil and process again until chopped. Add the tomatoes and pulse 3 or 4 times, leaving the tomatoes chunky. Season with the salt and pepper. Serve the sauce over the warm penne.

Yield: 6 to 8 servings

Note: Canned tomatoes may be substituted for the fresh ones. Serve this dish as an entrée or a side dish.

Vermicelli with Sun-Dried Tomatoes and Artichoke Hearts

*16 ounces vermicelli, cooked and
   drained*
*8 ounces marinated sun-dried
   tomatoes, chopped*
*6 ounces marinated artichoke
   hearts, drained and chopped*
8 ounces blue cheese, crumbled
*1 small bunch fresh basil (about
   9 leaves), torn*
*1/2 cup coarsely chopped walnuts,
   toasted (optional)*
Dash of cayenne pepper

Combine the hot pasta, sun-dried tomatoes, artichoke hearts, blue cheese and 1/2 of the basil in a large bowl and mix well. Remove to a serving platter. Sprinkle with the remaining basil, walnuts and cayenne pepper.

Yield: 6 to 8 servings

Note: Serve with a green salad and a loaf of fresh Italian bread for a perfect and quick dinner.

131

Italian Spinach Torta

2 prepared pie pastries
Flour
1 (10-ounce) package frozen
*   chopped spinach, thawed and*
*   squeezed dry*
2 cups ricotta cheese
$1/2$ cup (2 ounces) grated Parmesan
*   cheese*
2 cups (8 ounces) shredded
*   mozzarella cheese*
$1/4$ teaspoon garlic salt
$1/4$ teaspoon pepper
1 egg, separated
1 teaspoon water
Marinara sauce

Unfold 1 pastry and sprinkle with a little flour. Rub the flour over the pastry. Fit the pastry floured side down into a 10-inch tart pan with a removable bottom or into a 9-inch pie plate. Combine the spinach, ricotta cheese, Parmesan cheese, mozzarella cheese, garlic salt, pepper and egg yolk in a bowl and mix well. Spoon into the pie shell. Cut the remaining pastry into $3/4$-inch-wide strips, using a fluted pastry cutter or pizza wheel. Arrange lattice-fashion over the spinach mixture; trim and seal the edges. Whisk the egg white and water in a small bowl. Brush over the pastry. Bake at 400 degrees for 45 to 50 minutes or until golden brown. Let stand for 10 to 15 minutes. Serve with warmed marinara sauce.

Yield: 6 to 8 servings

132

Polenta Pie with Mushrooms and Spinach

1 pound white mushrooms, sliced
1 tablespoon olive oil
1/2 cup (2 ounces) freshly grated
  Parmesan cheese
1 (10-ounce) package frozen
  chopped spinach, thawed and
  squeezed dry
1/4 cup pesto
1 cup instant polenta or cornmeal
Marinara sauce
Pesto

Sauté the mushrooms in the olive oil in a skillet for 10 minutes or until light brown. Remove 1 cup of the mushrooms to a small bowl; stir in 1 tablespoon of the cheese. Add the spinach and 1/4 cup pesto to the mushrooms in the skillet. Cook for 2 minutes or until hot. Prepare the polenta according to the package directions. Remove from the heat. Stir in the remaining cheese. Spread 1/2 of the polenta in a 9-inch pie plate coated with nonstick cooking spray. Continue layering with the spinach-mushroom mixture, the remaining polenta, and the mushroom-cheese mixture. Bake at 375 degrees for 10 minutes. Let stand for 5 minutes. Cut into wedges. Serve on a bed of marinara sauce and top with a dollop of pesto.

Yield: 4 to 6 servings

Note: Make the pie ahead and chill, covered with foil, for up to 24 hours. To reheat, bake at 375 degrees for 30 minutes or until heated through.

133

Chocolate Walnut Biscotti

*1/2 cup (1 stick) butter or margarine,
  softened*
3/4 cup sugar
2 eggs
1 teaspoon vanilla extract
2 cups flour
1 1/2 teaspoons baking powder
1/4 teaspoon salt
*2/3 cup semisweet chocolate chips
  or chunks*
1 cup chopped walnuts

Cream the butter and sugar in a mixing bowl until light and fluffy. Beat in the eggs and vanilla. Add the flour, baking powder and salt and mix well. Stir in the chocolate chips and walnuts. Divide the dough into 2 equal portions. Shape into 1 1/2×14-inch logs and slightly flatten them. Place on a greased and floured cookie sheet. Bake at 325 degrees for 25 minutes or until light brown. Remove the logs to a cutting board. Cool for 5 minutes. Slice on a sharp diagonal with a serrated knife into 3/4-inch pieces. Stand the biscotti upright on the baking sheet 1/2 inch apart. Bake for 10 minutes or until slightly dry. Cool on a wire rack.

Yield: 3 dozen

Note: Try this recipe with butterscotch, white chocolate or other flavored chips.

134

Pizzelles

1 cup (2 sticks) butter, melted and
    cooled
1 1/2 cups sugar
6 eggs
2 teaspoons vanilla extract
2 to 3 drops of anise oil
2 tablespoons anise seeds
2 cups flour

Beat the butter, sugar, eggs, vanilla, anise oil and anise seeds in a mixing bowl. Stir in the flour gradually. Coat a heated pizzelle maker with nonstick cooking spray. Spoon the batter, 1 teaspoon at a time, on each side. Cook for 1 minute. Remove with a fork and cool on a wire rack.

Yield: 3 dozen

Dessert Pizza

1 roll refrigerator sugar cookie
    dough
8 ounces cream cheese, softened
1/2 cup sugar
Assorted fruit such as strawberries,
    blueberries, kiwifruit, seedless
    grapes and mandarin oranges

Spread the cookie dough on a cookie sheet. Bake at 350 degrees until light brown. Let cool completely. Beat the cream cheese and sugar in a mixing bowl. Spread over the cooled cookie dough. Top with a layer of fruit. Chill until serving time. Cut into wedges or squares.

Yield: 8 to 10 servings

Note: Be creative and match the colors of your fruit to your holiday decorating theme.

135

A Concert of Confections

From the sweet sounds of Bach and Beethoven to the foot stompin' beat of the latest country hits, Wheeling is the setting for a mosaic of music and has a definite flair for entertainment.

The Wheeling Symphony Orchestra offers both classical and pop concerts as well as its holiday spectacular, Symphony on Ice. Every Fourth of July and Labor Day, the WSO takes its show out under the stars in and around Wheeling, showcasing the Heritage Port and Oglebay Park free to the public.

For the last 70 years, the Capitol Music Hall has hosted one of the premier country music programs in America, Jamboree USA. Each Saturday night, the Jamboree has brought the hottest names in country music "from the heart of America to America's heart." The Capitol Music Hall has also played host to nationally touring Broadway musicals, bringing the magic of the Big Apple to the heartland.

One cannot forget to mention The Superbowl of Country Music, Jamboree in the Hills. The four-day country concert is a nationally known and recognized extravaganza that brings everyone, both young and old alike, together to party in the hills and celebrate with music.

From tantalizing sounds for all tastes to delectable desserts to tempt any palate, the Ohio Valley has great taste. ENCORE!

"The Capitol Music Hall" by Joyce Patterson. An Ohio Valley native who has "always wanted to draw" is thrilled to share that desire with others in her art classes. Mrs. Patterson is happiest capturing the area closest to her heart and her roots, Wheeling. She has "happy memories of coming to the city" and tries to recreate that feeling in her work. She succeeded so well that country music star Brad Paisley displays this piece in his home.

Butterscotch Cake

1 (2-layer) package yellow cake mix
1/3 cup vegetable oil
3 eggs
1 can Thank You butterscotch
    pudding
2 2/3 cups butterscotch chips

Combine the cake mix, oil, eggs and pudding in a bowl and mix well. Pour into a greased and floured 9×13-inch baking pan. Bake at 350 degrees for 15 minutes. Sprinkle the butterscotch chips evenly over the baked layer. Bake for 30 minutes longer or until the cake tests done.

Yield: 12 to 15 servings

Note: This cake is definitely for butterscotch lovers.

Dust-Free Baking
Are you tired of that white dusty residue that clings to your cakes from the flour-dusted pans? Try this:
Dust your greased pan with some of the dry cake mix being prepared. Bake your cake in the pan and enjoy
a cleaner, sweeter treat!

139

Perfectly Chocolate Cake

2 cups sugar
1³/4 cups flour
³/4 cup baking cocoa
1¹/2 teaspoons baking powder
1¹/2 teaspoons baking soda
1 teaspoon salt
2 eggs
1 cup milk
¹/2 cup vegetable oil
2 teaspoons vanilla extract
1 cup boiling water
Favorite chocolate frosting

Combine the sugar, flour, baking cocoa, baking powder, baking soda and salt in a mixing bowl. Add the eggs, milk, oil and vanilla. Beat for 2 minutes or until smooth. Stir in the boiling water and mix well. Pour into 3 greased and floured 8-inch cake pans. Bake at 350 degrees for 18 to 23 minutes or until the layers test done. Cool in the pans for 10 minutes. Remove to wire racks to cool completely. Spread favorite chocolate frosting between the layers and over the top and side of the cake.

Yield: 10 to 12 servings

140

Hand-Me-Down Cake

3/4 cup shortening or softened
  margarine
1 3/4 cups sugar
2 eggs
1 teaspoon vanilla extract
2 cups flour
3/4 cup baking cocoa
1 1/4 teaspoons baking soda
1 teaspoon salt
1 1/3 cups water
Favorite frosting

Cream the shortening and sugar in a mixing bowl until light and fluffy. Add the eggs and vanilla. Beat for 1 minute. Combine the flour, baking cocoa, baking soda and salt in a bowl. Add to the creamed mixture alternately with the water, mixing well after each addition. Pour into a greased and floured 9×13-inch cake pan. Bake at 350 degrees for 35 to 45 minutes or until the cake tests done. Let cool and then frost with favorite frosting.

Yield: 15 servings

Sugar Cookie Cake

3 cups flour
2 cups sugar
3/4 cup (1 1/2 sticks) margarine,
  softened
1 1/2 cups buttermilk
1 teaspoon baking soda
2 eggs
1 teaspoon vanilla extract

Combine the flour and sugar in a bowl. Cut in the margarine until crumbly. Reserve 1 cup for the topping. Stir a mixture of the buttermilk and baking soda into the remaining flour mixture. Beat in the eggs and vanilla. Pour into a greased and floured 9×13-inch cake pan. Sprinkle with the reserved flour mixture. Bake at 350 degrees for 30 to 40 minutes or until the cake tests done.

Yield: 12 servings

141

Lemon Poppy Seed Cake

8 ounces cream cheese, softened
1/2 cup (1 stick) butter, softened
2 cups sugar
2 tablespoons grated lemon zest
4 eggs
2 teaspoons vanilla extract
3 cups flour
1/3 cup poppy seeds
1 1/4 teaspoons baking powder
3/4 teaspoon baking soda
1/2 teaspoon salt
1/3 cup milk

Combine the cream cheese, butter, sugar and lemon zest in a mixing bowl. Beat at low speed until well mixed. Beat at medium-high speed for 3 minutes longer or until smooth and creamy. Add the eggs 1 at a time, beating well after each addition. Add the vanilla. Combine the flour, poppy seeds, baking powder, baking soda and salt in a bowl. Add to the creamed mixture alternately with the milk, beginning and ending with the milk. Beat until smooth. Pour into a greased and floured bundt pan. Bake at 325 degrees for 55 to 65 minutes or until the cake tests done. Cool in the pan for 15 minutes. Invert onto a wire rack to cool completely.

Yield: 20 servings

142

Apple Pie with Crumb Topping

7 to 9 tart apples, peeled and sliced
1/2 cup sugar
1/2 teaspoon cinnamon
1 unbaked (9-inch) pie shell
Crumb Topping

Toss the apples with the sugar and cinnamon in a bowl. Spoon into the pie shell. Sprinkle with the Crumb Topping. Bake at 400 degrees for 40 to 60 minutes or until golden brown.

Yield: 8 to 10 servings

CRUMB TOPPING

3/4 cup flour
1/2 cup sugar
1/3 to 1/2 cup butter

Combine the flour and sugar in a bowl. Cut in the butter until crumbly.

Oreo Cookie Mousse Pie

1 package Oreo cookie pie shell
    mix
1 (6-ounce) package chocolate
    instant pudding mix
2 cups milk
16 ounces whipped topping
12 (or more) Oreo cookies, crushed
6 ounces chocolate chips

Prepare the pie shell using the package directions. Combine the pudding mix and milk in a bowl and mix well. Chill for 15 minutes. Fold in 1 or 2 cups whipped topping to make a mousse-like texture, reserving the remaining whipped topping. Fold in the crushed cookies and 1 or 2 handfuls of the chocolate chips. Spoon into the pie shell. Spread with the reserved whipped topping. Garnish with additional cookie crumbs and remaining chocolate chips.

Yield: 6 to 8 servings

143

S'more Tarts

1 package fudge brownie mix
12 graham cracker tart shells
1¹/₂ cups miniature marshmallows
6 ounces chocolate chips

Prepare the brownie mix using the package directions. Spoon into the tart shells. Arrange the tarts on a baking sheet. Bake at 350 degrees for 25 to 35 minutes or until a wooden pick brings out moist crumbs. Sprinkle with the marshmallows and chocolate chips. Bake for 5 to 10 minutes longer or until golden brown.

Yield: 12 tarts

Note: This filling may be baked in a 9-inch graham cracker pie shell. For bite-size servings, make 1-inch graham cracker shells in miniature muffin cups and use 1 large marshmallow along with chocolate chips for the topping of each serving.

144

Apple Crisp

5 or 6 apples, peeled, sliced
1 cup sifted flour
1 cup (or less) sugar
1 teaspoon baking powder
³/4 teaspoon salt
1 egg
¹/3 cup margarine, melted
Cinnamon

Place the apples in a deep 6×10-inch baking dish. Combine the flour, sugar, baking powder, salt and egg in a bowl and mix until crumbly. Sprinkle over the apples. Drizzle the margarine over the top. Sprinkle with cinnamon. Bake at 350 degrees for 40 to 45 minutes or until brown and bubbly. Serve warm with ice cream.

Yield: 4 to 5 servings

Note: The amount of sugar needed depends on the tartness of the apples.

Banana Split Dessert

2 cups confectioners' sugar
¹/2 cup (1 stick) butter, softened
1 egg
1 teaspoon vanilla extract
2 (9-inch) graham cracker pie shells
4 bananas, sliced
2 (20-ounce) cans crushed
   pineapple, drained
16 ounces whipped topping
Chopped nuts (optional)
Maraschino cherries (optional)

Beat the confectioners' sugar, butter, egg and vanilla in a mixing bowl. Spread in the pie shells. Layer the banana slices, crushed pineapple and whipped topping over the creamy layers. Sprinkle with nuts and cherries. Chill for at least 2 hours.

Yield: 12 to 16 servings

Note: To avoid raw eggs that may carry salmonella, we suggest using an equivalent amount of pasteurized egg substitute.

145

Cream Puff Dessert

1 cup water
1/2 cup (1 stick) butter
1 cup flour
4 eggs
2 (3-ounce) packages vanilla instant
    pudding mix
8 ounces cream cheese, softened
3 1/2 cups milk
16 ounces whipped topping

Bring the water and butter to a boil in a saucepan. Add the flour and cook over low heat for 1 minute or until the mixture forms a ball, stirring vigorously. Remove from the heat. Beat in the eggs 1 at a time; continue beating until smooth and glossy. Spread in a 9×13-inch baking pan. Bake at 350 degrees for 20 to 25 minutes or until puffed and brown. Cool completely. Combine the pudding mix, cream cheese and milk in a bowl and mix well. Spread over the cooled crust. Top with the whipped topping.

Yield: 10 servings

Miniature Cheesecakes

16 ounces cream cheese, softened
1 cup sugar
2 eggs
1/2 teaspoon vanilla extract
18 vanilla wafers
1 can favorite pie filling

Combine the cream cheese, sugar, eggs and vanilla in a mixing bowl and blend well. Place a vanilla wafer in each of 18 foil-lined muffin cups. Fill 2/3 full with the cream cheese mixture. Bake at 375 degrees for 10 to 15 minutes or until the tops are dry. Spoon a small amount of favorite pie filling over each cheesecake. Chill until serving time.

Yield: 18 cheesecakes

146

Frosted Banana Bars

*1/2 cup (1 stick) butter or margarine,
   softened*
2 cups sugar
3 eggs
*1 1/2 cups mashed bananas (about 3
   bananas)*
1 teaspoon vanilla extract
2 cups flour
1 teaspoon baking soda
Pinch of salt
Cream Cheese Frosting

Cream the butter and sugar in a mixing bowl until light and fluffy. Add the eggs 1 at a time, mixing well after each addition. Stir in the bananas and vanilla. Combine the flour, baking soda and salt in a bowl. Add to the creamed mixture gradually, mixing well after each addition. Pour into a greased and floured 10×15-inch baking pan. Bake at 350 degrees for 25 minutes or until golden brown. Cool completely. Spread with the Cream Cheese Frosting. Cut into bars. Store, tightly wrapped, in the refrigerator.

Yield: 3 dozen bars

Note: A blender works well for mashing the bananas. This recipe is great for picnics and entertaining because of the large quantity it makes.

CREAM CHEESE FROSTING

*1/2 cup (1 stick) butter or margarine,
   softened*
8 ounces cream cheese, softened
4 cups confectioners' sugar
2 teaspoons vanilla extract

Beat the butter and cream cheese in a mixing bowl until smooth. Add the confectioners' sugar and vanilla gradually, beating well after each addition.

147

Chess Pie Squares

1 cup flour
$1/2$ cup (1 stick) butter, softened
3 tablespoons sugar
1 cup packed brown sugar
$1/2$ cup sugar
1 tablespoon flour
3 eggs, lightly beaten
3 tablespoons butter, melted
$1/2$ teaspoon vanilla extract
Chopped pecans (optional)

Combine 1 cup flour, $1/2$ cup butter and 3 tablespoons sugar in a bowl and blend well. Press evenly in an 8×8-inch baking pan. Bake at 350 degrees for 15 to 20 minutes or until light brown. Combine the brown sugar, $1/2$ cup sugar and 1 tablespoon flour in a bowl. Add the eggs and mix well. Stir in the melted butter gradually. Add the vanilla and mix well. Pour over the baked crust. Sprinkle with pecans. Bake at 350 degrees for 25 to 30 minutes or until light brown and set. Cool completely. Cut into squares.

Yield: 2 dozen squares

Festive Fudge-Filled Bars

2 cups quick-cooking oats
1¹/₂ cups flour
1 cup chopped nuts
1 cup packed brown sugar
1 teaspoon baking soda
³/₄ teaspoon salt
1 cup (2 sticks) butter or margarine,
  melted
2 tablespoons shortening
1 cup "M & M's" Plain Chocolate
  Candies
1 (14-ounce) can sweetened
  condensed milk
¹/₂ cup "M & M's" Plain Chocolate
  Candies

Combine the oats, flour, nuts, brown sugar, baking soda and salt in a bowl. Add the butter and mix until crumbly. Reserve 1¹/₂ cups for the topping. Press the remaining oat mixture into a greased 9×13-inch baking pan. Bake at 375 degrees for 10 minutes. Melt the shortening in a saucepan over low heat. Stir in 1 cup candy and crush with the back of a spoon. Cook until the chocolate is melted, leaving bits of the color coating visible. Remove from the heat. Stir in the condensed milk. Spread over the baked layer to within ¹/₂ inch of the edges. Mix the reserved oat mixture and ¹/₂ cup candy in a bowl. Sprinkle over the chocolate layer, pressing the candy into the chocolate layer. Bake for 20 minutes or until golden brown. Cool completely. Cut into bars.

Yield: 4 dozen bars

149

Oatmeal Extravaganzas

1 cup plus 2 tablespoons packed
    brown sugar
3/4 cup (1 1/2 sticks) butter, softened
2 teaspoons vanilla extract
1 cup plus 2 tablespoons flour
1 1/2 teaspoons baking powder
1/2 teaspoon salt
1/4 cup water
2 cups quick-cooking oats
12 ounces chocolate chips

Cream the brown sugar, butter and vanilla in a mixing bowl until light and fluffy. Combine the flour, baking powder and salt in a bowl. Add to the creamed mixture alternately with the water. Stir in the oats and chocolate chips. Spread in a greased 9×9-inch baking pan. Bake at 375 degrees for 30 minutes. Cool on a wire rack. Cut into squares.

Yield: 16 squares

Hello Dolly Squares

1/2 cup (1 stick) butter, softened
1 cup graham cracker crumbs
1 cup shredded unsweetened
    coconut
1 cup chocolate chips
1 cup chopped nuts
1 (14-ounce) can sweetened
    condensed milk

Melt the butter in an 8×8-inch baking pan. Layer with the graham cracker crumbs, coconut, chocolate chips and nuts. Pour the sweetened condensed milk evenly over the top. Bake at 350 degrees for 30 minutes. Let stand to cool slightly. Cut into squares. You may double the ingredients and bake in a 9×13-inch baking pan.

Yield: 9 squares

150

Jewish Cookies

3/4 cup (1 1/2) sticks butter, softened
1 1/4 cups sugar
3 eggs
1 cup flour
3 tablespoons baking cocoa
1/4 teaspoon salt
1 cup nuts, crushed
7 ounces shredded coconut
1 (14-ounce) can sweetened
    condensed milk
1 can milk chocolate frosting

Beat the butter, sugar and eggs in a mixing bowl. Add the flour, baking cocoa and salt and mix well. Spread on a greased cookie sheet. Sprinkle with the crushed nuts. Bake at 350 degrees for 15 minutes. Combine the coconut and condensed milk in a bowl and mix well. Spread over the baked layer. Bake for 15 minutes longer. Cool on a wire rack. Frost with the chocolate frosting. Cut into bars or squares.

Yield: 40 cookies

Peanut Butter Jumbos

1/2 cup (1 stick) butter, softened
1 cup packed brown sugar
1 cup sugar
1 1/2 cups peanut butter
3 eggs
4 1/2 cups rolled oats
2 teaspoons baking soda
1 teaspoon vanilla extract
6 ounces semisweet chocolate
    chips
1 cup "M & M's" Chocolate Candies

Cream the butter, brown sugar, sugar, peanut butter and eggs in a bowl until light and fluffy. Add the oats, baking soda and vanilla and mix well. Stir in the chocolate chips and candy. Drop by 1/3 cupfuls 4 inches apart onto a nonstick cookie sheet. Flatten slightly. Bake at 350 degrees for 15 to 20 minutes or until firm in the center. Cool on a wire rack.

Yield: 1 dozen cookies

151

Chewy Surprise Cookies

1¹/₂ cups butter-flavor shortening
1¹/₂ cups peanut butter
1¹/₂ cups sugar
1¹/₂ cups packed brown sugar
4 eggs
3³/₄ cups flour
2 teaspoons baking soda
1¹/₂ teaspoons baking powder
³/₄ teaspoon salt
1 (10-ounce) package Milk Duds
¹/₂ cup sugar

Cream the shortening, peanut butter, 1¹/₂ cups sugar and brown sugar in a mixing bowl until light and fluffy. Add the eggs 1 at a time, beating well after each addition. Combine the flour, baking soda, baking powder and salt in a bowl. Add to the creamed mixture and mix well. Chill for at least 1 hour. Shape 2 teaspoons of the dough around each Milk Dud, completely covering the candy. Roll in the ¹/₂ cup sugar. Place 2 inches apart on an ungreased cookie sheet. Bake at 350 degrees for 10 to 12 minutes or until set. Cool for 5 minutes. Remove to a wire rack to cool completely.

Yield: 8 dozen cookies

Note: These cookies will keep everyone guessing what is inside.

152

Chocolate Chip Cookies

1 cup sugar
1 cup packed brown sugar
1 cup (2 sticks) butter or margarine,
   softened
2 eggs
1¹/₂ teaspoons vanilla extract
3 cups flour
1 teaspoon salt
1 teaspoon baking soda
12 ounces semisweet chocolate
   chips

Combine the sugar, brown sugar, butter, eggs and vanilla in a mixing bowl. Beat at low speed for 30 seconds. Scrape down the sides. Beat at medium speed for 30 seconds. Sift the flour, salt and baking soda together. Add gradually to the sugar mixture, beating constantly at low speed. Beat for 2 minutes. Beat at medium speed for 2 minutes. Stir in the chocolate chips. Chill, covered, for 30 to 60 minutes. Drop by teaspoonfuls 2 inches apart onto greased cookie sheets. Bake at 375 degrees for 10 to 12 minutes or until golden brown.

Yield: 3¹/₂ dozen

153

Russian Tea Cakes

1 cup (2 sticks) butter
$^1/_2$ cup confectioners' sugar
1 teaspoon vanilla extract
$2^1/_4$ cups flour
$^1/_4$ teaspoon salt
$^3/_4$ cup finely chopped nuts
Confectioners' sugar

Cream the butter, $^1/_2$ cup confectioners' sugar and vanilla in a mixing bowl until light and fluffy. Mix in the flour and salt. Add the nuts. Chill for 10 to 30 minutes. Shape the dough into 1-inch balls. Place 2 inches apart on an ungreased cookie sheet. Bake at 400 degrees for 10 to 12 minutes or until set but not brown. Roll the warm cookies in confectioners' sugar. Cool on a wire rack. Roll the cookies in confectioners' sugar again before serving.

Yield: 3 to 4 dozen cookies

154

Mom's Butter Cookies

³/4 cup (1¹/2 sticks) salted butter
¹/2 cup packed brown sugar
1 tablespoon sugar
1 egg yolk, unbeaten
1 teaspoon vanilla extract
2 cups flour
Butter Icing

Cream the butter in a mixing bowl until light and fluffy. Beat in the brown sugar, sugar, egg yolk and vanilla. Add the flour and mix well. Chill for at least 1 hour. Roll the dough ¹/4 inch thick on a floured surface. Cut into desired shapes. Place on a nonstick cookie sheet. Bake at 350 degrees for 7 to 9 minutes or until light brown. Cool on a wire rack. Frost the cooled cookies with the Butter Icing.

Yield: 2 to 3 dozen cookies

Note: Real butter is an absolute must in these cookies.

BUTTER ICING

¹/4 cup (¹/2 stick) butter
2¹/2 cups confectioners' sugar
1 teaspoon vanilla extract
1 tablespoon evaporated milk
Food coloring of choice (optional)

Melt the butter in a saucepan or brown the butter if no food coloring will be used. Remove from the heat. Add the confectioners' sugar and vanilla and mix well. Stir in the evaporated milk a few drops at a time. Stir in food coloring as desired.

155

Kathi's Sugar Cookies

1 cup (2 sticks) butter, softened
1 cup vegetable oil
1 cup sugar
1 cup confectioners' sugar
2 eggs
1 teaspoon vanilla extract
4 cups plus 2 tablespoons flour
1 teaspoon baking soda
1 teaspoon cream of tartar
1 teaspoon salt
Sugar
Sugar Cookie Icing

Cream the butter, oil, sugar, confectioners' sugar, eggs and vanilla in a mixing bowl until light and fluffy. Combine the flour, baking soda, cream of tartar and salt in a bowl. Add to the creamed mixture and mix well. Shape the dough into small balls. Place 2 inches apart on a nonstick cookie sheet. Flatten with a glass dipped into additional sugar. Bake at 350 degrees for 10 to 12 minutes or until the edges are golden brown. Cool on a wire rack.
Frost the cooled cookies with the Sugar Cookie Icing.

Yield: 4 to 5 dozen cookies

SUGAR COOKIE ICING

Confectioners' sugar
Water
Food coloring (optional)

Combine confectioners' sugar, a few drops of water and a few drops of food coloring in a bowl and mix well. Add more water for a thin icing to drizzle over cookies. Add less water for a spreadable icing.

Vanilla Chip Maple Cookies

1 cup shortening
1/2 cup (1 stick) butter, softened
2 cups packed brown sugar
2 eggs
1 teaspoon vanilla extract
1 teaspoon maple flavoring
3 cups flour
2 teaspoons baking soda
2 cups (12 ounces) vanilla chips or
    white chocolate chips
1/2 cup chopped pecans
Maple Frosting
3 1/2 cups pecan halves

Cream the shortening, butter and brown sugar in a mixing bowl until light and fluffy. Add the eggs 1 at a time, beating well after each addition. Stir in the vanilla and maple flavoring. Combine the flour and baking soda in a bowl. Add to the creamed mixture gradually, mixing well after each addition. Stir in the vanilla chips and 1/2 cup pecans. Drop the dough by rounded tablespoonfuls 2 inches apart onto an ungreased cookie sheet. Bake at 350 degrees for 8 to 10 minutes or until golden brown. Cool for 2 minutes. Remove to a wire rack to cool completely. Frost the cooled cookies with the Maple Frosting. Top each with a pecan half.

Yield: 7 dozen cookies

MAPLE FROSTING

1/4 cup (1/2 stick) butter, softened
4 cups confectioners' sugar
1 teaspoon maple flavoring
4 to 6 tablespoons milk

Cream the butter and confectioners' sugar in a mixing bowl until light and fluffy. Add the maple flavoring and enough milk to make of spreading consistency.

157

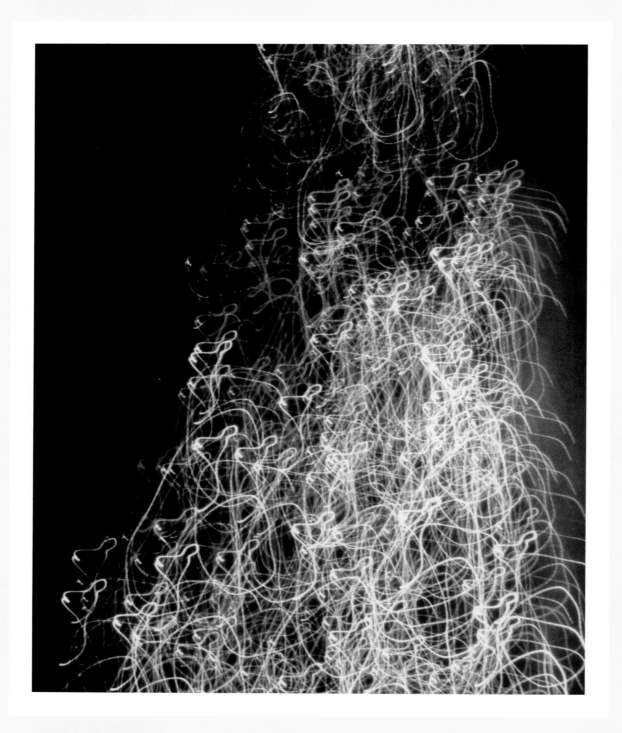

Magical Holidays

Christmas in the Ohio Valley is a magical time as communities are ablaze with thousands of lights and sounds that permeate the air.

Oglebay Park's Winter Festival of Lights is one of the nation's largest light shows, covering more than 300 acres over a six-mile drive throughout the resort. Downtown Wheeling features dozens of homes, shops, and businesses illuminated in celebration of the city's designation as the "City of Lights." The annual Christmas parades in every town, city, and village, and the Wheeling Symphony's Holiday on Ice, bring the sounds of the winter wonderland to every resident and visitor alike.

Other holiday celebrations include West Virginia Day, which celebrates the state's place as the 35th star on the American flag, held every June 29th at Independence Hall, the state's previous capitol building. The Fourth of July at Heritage Port includes music, fun, food, and a fabulous fireworks display that rounds out a true Ohio Valley commemoration of our nation's birthday. In fact, in just about every town around, you'll find elaborate "birthday parties" to enjoy.

No holiday would be complete without the magic of good eats. And if you've ever visited the Ohio Valley, you know we have a flair for making any holiday a magical one.

Using a unique photographic technique, "Light Drawing" is Sandra Hadsell's imagination at work with a Christmas tree. As an art specialist for the Marshall County School System, Mrs. Hadsell adores educating young elementary-age children about art and life. She encourages her students to "find their passion, as we all are artists of some form, and to look for their happy accidents, as there are no mistakes in art."

Shawn Turak

Wassail

6 cups apple juice
2 cups cranberry juice cocktail
1 cup water
¼ cup packed brown sugar
2 cinnamon sticks
20 whole cloves in a tea ball

Combine the apple juice, cranberry juice cocktail, water, brown sugar, cinnamon sticks and cloves in a saucepan. Bring to a boil. Serve hot.

Yield: 8 servings

Warm Up to These Holiday Drinks

Candy Cane Cocoa: Heat 4 cups milk in a saucepan until hot but not boiling. Add 3 ounces semisweet chocolate and 4 crushed peppermint candy canes. Cook until melted and smooth, stirring constantly. Pour into mugs. Top each with about ¼ cup whipped cream and add a peppermint candy cane to stir. Yield: 4 servings.

Hot Raspberry Cider: Combine 8 cups apple cider, 1 cup thawed frozen raspberry juice concentrate, 1 tablespoon sugar and 1 cinnamon stick in a saucepan. Bring to a boil over medium heat. Reduce the heat and simmer for 10 minutes. Remove the cinnamon stick and pour into mugs. Yield: 8 to 10 servings.

Hot Buttered Rum Mix: Cream 1 cup softened unsalted butter, 1 (1-pound) package confectioners' sugar and 1 (1-pound) package brown sugar in a mixing bowl until light and fluffy. Add 1 quart softened vanilla ice cream and mix to a creamy consistency. Transfer to a freezer container with a tight-fitting lid. Freeze for up to 1 month. To serve, spoon 2 tablespoons frozen mixture into a mug or heatproof glass. Add 1 to 2 tablespoons dark rum. Pour 6 ounces boiling water over the mixture and stir until melted. Garnish with cinnamon or nutmeg if desired. Yield: about 20 servings.

White Hot Chocolate

6 cups milk
2 cups heavy cream
12 ounces white chocolate,
*   finely chopped*
1 teaspoon vanilla extract

Heat the milk and cream in a saucepan over medium heat until bubbles form around the edge. Pour over the white chocolate in a heatproof bowl or saucepan. Stir until melted. Whisk in the vanilla.

Yield: 8 servings

Golden Party Punch

1 (2-liter) bottle ginger ale
1 quart white grape juice

Combine the ginger ale and grape juice in a punch bowl and mix well.

Yield: about 25 servings

Note: This recipe can be doubled. Vary the amounts of ginger ale and grape juice to suit your taste. Serve as a Golden Anniversary punch.

Champagne with Punch

Champagne
2 ounces Chambord liqueur
Lemon-lime soda

Fill a Champagne glass $1/2$ full with champagne. Add 2 ounces liqueur. Add enough lemon-lime soda to fill the glass.

Yield: 1 serving

Blue Cheese Ball

8 ounces cream cheese, softened
2 tablespoons parsley
2 ounces blue cheese, crumbled
$1/4$ cup chopped onion
3 tablespoons chopped celery
2 tablespoons dried chives
   (optional)

Combine the cream cheese, parsley, blue cheese, onion, celery and chives in a bowl and mix well. Shape into a ball. Chill until serving time. Serve with crackers.

Yield: 10 to 12 servings

Cheese Ball

24 ounces cream cheese, softened
1 (5-ounce) jar Old English cheese
   spread
1 (5-ounce) jar Reka, or 5 ounces
   blue cheese
1 garlic clove, minced
2 cups chopped walnuts or pecans

Combine the cream cheese, cheese spread, Reka and garlic in a bowl and mix well. Shape into a ball. Chill for 2 hours. Roll in the chopped walnuts. Serve with crackers.

Yield: 15 to 20 servings

Corn Casserole

1 (14-ounce) can whole kernel corn
1 (14-ounce) can cream-style corn
1/2 cup (1 stick) butter or margarine
1 (8-ounce) package corn
   muffin mix
1 egg
1 cup sour cream

Combine the whole kernel corn, cream-style corn, butter, corn muffin mix, egg and sour cream in a bowl and mix well. Pour into a greased 8×8-inch casserole. Bake at 350 degrees for 1 hour.

Yield: 4 to 6 servings

Sweet Potato Casserole

2 cups canned yams, mashed
$1/4$ cup sugar
2 eggs
$1/4$ cup ($1/2$ stick) butter
$1/2$ cup milk
$1/2$ teaspoon cinnamon
$1/4$ teaspoon nutmeg
Crispy Topping

Combine the yams, sugar, eggs, butter and milk in a bowl and mix well. Stir in the cinnamon and nutmeg. Bake at 350 degrees for 20 minutes. Spread the Crispy Topping over the casserole. Bake at 200 degrees for 10 minutes longer.

Yield: 6 servings

CRISPY TOPPING

6 tablespoons butter
$1/2$ cup packed brown sugar
$3/4$ cup crisp rice cereal
$1/2$ cup chopped pecans

Combine the butter and brown sugar in a saucepan. Cook over low heat until the butter melts, stirring constantly. Stir in the cereal and pecans.

Pinwheel

1 (10-ounce) package frozen
   spinach, cooked and
   squeezed dry
1/2 cup bread crumbs
1/2 cup (2 ounces) grated Parmesan
   cheese
1/4 cup olive oil
2 garlic cloves, minced
4 to 6 thin slices prosciutto or boiled
   ham
1 (1 1/2-pound) flank steak, trimmed
2 tablespoons olive oil

Combine the spinach, bread crumbs, cheese, 1/4 cup olive oil and garlic in a food processor and process until the ingredients form a paste. Layer the prosciutto and the spinach paste over the flank steak. Roll up the steak from the narrow end. Rub with 2 tablespoons olive oil. Tie the steak roll securely with kitchen string. Place on a rack in a roasting pan. Bake at 375 degrees for 35 to 40 minutes or to 160 degrees on a meat thermometer for medium. Let stand for a few minutes before slicing.

Yield: 4 to 6 servings

Wild Turkey Pork Roast

1 (3-pound) pork roast
Juice of 1 lemon
1 heaping tablespoon light brown
   sugar
1 teaspoon flour
1 teaspoon paprika
1/2 teaspoon salt
Fresh ground pepper
1/4 cup water
1/4 cup Wild Turkey Bourbon
1/4 cup cooking sherry
Chopped fresh parsley
1 bay leaf
1/4 cup Wild Turkey Bourbon

Rub the roast with the lemon juice. Combine the brown sugar, flour, paprika and salt and mix well. Rub the roast with the brown sugar mixture. Sprinkle with the pepper. Place in a roasting pan. Combine the water, 1/4 cup bourbon and sherry in a bowl and mix well. Pour carefully over the roast. Sprinkle with the parsley. Place the bay leaf in the pan. Bake at 350 degrees for 1 1/4 hours, basting frequently with pan drippings. Pour the remaining bourbon over the roast. Bake for 1 hour longer or to desired degree of doneness.

Yield: 8 servings

Pecan Chicken

¹/₂ cup (1 stick) butter
1 cup buttermilk
1 egg, lightly beaten
1 cup flour
1 cup ground pecans
Salt to taste
1 tablespoon paprika
¹/₈ teaspoon pepper
¹/₄ cup sesame seeds
2 (2¹/₂-pound) chickens,
   cut into quarters or pieces
¹/₄ cup pecan halves

Melt the butter in a 10×15-inch baking dish. Whisk the buttermilk and egg in a shallow bowl. Mix the flour, ground pecans, salt, paprika, pepper and sesame seeds on a plate. Dip the chicken in the buttermilk mixture. Coat with the flour mixture. Place skin side down in the melted butter. Turn the chicken skin side up. Sprinkle with the pecan halves. Bake at 350 degrees for 1¹/₄ hours or until cooked through and golden brown.

Yield: 8 servings

Bailey's Cheesecake

2 cups graham cracker crumbs
1/4 cup sugar
6 tablespoons butter, melted
36 ounces cream cheese, softened
1 2/3 cups sugar
2 eggs
1 cup Bailey's Irish cream
1 tablespoon vanilla extract
6 ounces semisweet chocolate
   chips
1 cup whipping cream, chilled
1 tablespoon sugar
1 teaspoon instant coffee powder

Combine the graham cracker crumbs and sugar in a bowl. Stir in the butter and mix until crumbly. Press the mixture into the bottom and up the side of a 9-inch springform pan coated with nonstick cooking spray. Bake at 325 degrees for 7 minutes or until light brown. Beat the cream cheese in a mixing bowl until smooth. Add the sugar gradually, beating well after each addition. Add the eggs 1 at a time, beating well after each addition. Stir in the Bailey's Irish cream and vanilla. Sprinkle 1/2 of the chocolate chips over the baked crust. Pour in the cream cheese filling. Sprinkle with the remaining chocolate chips. Bake at 325 degrees for 1 hour and 20 minutes or until puffed, springy in the center and golden brown. Cool completely. Chill until serving time. Combine the whipping cream, sugar and instant coffee powder in a mixing bowl. Beat until soft peaks form. Spread over the cooled cake or serve on the side.

Yield: 8 to 10 servings

Hummingbird Cake

3 cups flour
2 cups sugar
1 teaspoon baking soda
1 teaspoon cinnamon
1/2 teaspoon salt
3 eggs, beaten
3/4 cup vegetable oil
1 teaspoon vanilla extract
1 (8-ounce) can crushed pineapple
   with juice
3 medium bananas, mashed
1 cup chopped pecans
Cream Cheese Frosting
3 tablespoons chopped pecans

Combine the flour, sugar, baking soda, cinnamon and salt in a mixing bowl. Add the eggs, oil, vanilla, undrained pineapple, bananas and pecans and mix well. Pour into 3 greased and floured 9-inch cake pans. Bake at 350 degrees for 25 minutes or until the layers test done, rotating on the racks for even cooking. Cool in the pans for 10 minutes. Remove to wire racks to cool completely. Spread the Cream Cheese Frosting between the layers and over the top and side of the cooled cake. Sprinkle the pecans on top of the frosted cake.

Yield: 8 to 10 servings

Note: This cake works best when baked in 3 layers rather than as one large layer. Don't let the long list of ingredients in this recipe scare you away. It's well worth the effort.

CREAM CHEESE FROSTING

1/2 cup (1 stick) butter, softened
8 ounces cream cheese, softened
1 (1-pound) package confectioners'
   sugar
1/8 teaspoon vanilla extract
1/8 teaspoon lemon juice

Beat the butter and cream cheese in a mixing bowl. Add the confectioners' sugar gradually, beating well after each addition. Stir in the vanilla and lemon juice.

HoHo Cake

1 (2-layer) package chocolate cake
   mix
1¹/₂ cups milk
5 tablespoons flour
1 cup sugar
¹/₂ cup shortening
¹/₂ cup (1 stick) butter or margarine,
   softened
Chocolate Icing

*P*repare the cake mix using the package directions. Spread the batter on a greased and floured 9×13-inch baking pan and bake at the recommended temperature for 10 to 20 minutes or until the cake tests done. Cool. Whisk the milk into the flour in a saucepan. Cook over medium heat until thickened, stirring constantly. Let cool. Remove to a mixing bowl. Combine the sugar, shortening and butter in a bowl and mix well. Add to the cooled milk mixture. Beat for 5 minutes or until fluffy. Spread on the cooled cake. Freeze until hard. Spread the Chocolate Icing over the cream layer. Store in the refrigerator.

Yield: 12 to 15 servings

CHOCOLATE ICING

¹/₂ cup (1 stick) butter or margarine
1 egg
1 teaspoon vanilla extract
2¹/₂ tablespoons hot water
3 cups confectioners' sugar
3 ounces unsweetened chocolate,
   melted

Combine the butter, egg, vanilla, water, confectioners' sugar and chocolate in a mixing bowl. Beat until smooth.

Aunt Em's Harvest Cake

4 cups chopped peeled apples
2 cups sugar
3 cups flour
2 teaspoons baking soda
1/2 teaspoon salt
2 teaspoons vanilla extract
2 eggs, lightly beaten
1 cup vegetable oil
1 cup coarsely chopped walnuts
Coconut and Walnut Topping

Combine the apples and sugar in a bowl and mix well. Let stand for 1 hour before baking. Combine the flour, baking soda and salt. Add to the apples and mix well. Stir in the vanilla. Combine the eggs and oil in a mixing bowl. Beat until thick. Add to the apples and mix well. Stir in the walnuts. Pour into a 9×13-inch cake pan coated with nonstick cooking spray. Bake at 325 degrees for 50 minutes or until the cake tests done. Cool in the pan. Spread the Coconut and Walnut Topping over the cooled cake. Place under a broiler until the topping is light brown.

Yield: 8 to 10 servings

COCONUT AND WALNUT TOPPING

1 cup packed brown sugar
1 tablespoon heavy cream or half-
   and-half
1 cup shredded coconut
1/4 cup (1/2 stick) butter, melted
1/2 cup chopped walnuts

Combine the brown sugar, cream, coconut, butter and walnuts in a bowl and mix well.

Rum Cake

³/₄ cup chopped pecans
1 (2-layer) package yellow cake mix
1 (3-ounce) package vanilla instant
  pudding mix
¹/₂ cup rum
¹/₂ cup water
¹/₂ cup vegetable oil
4 eggs
Rum Sauce

Sprinkle the pecans in a greased and floured bundt, tube or 9×13-inch cake pan. Combine the cake mix, pudding mix, rum, water, oil and eggs in a bowl and mix well. Pour into the prepared pan. Bake at 325 degrees for 35 to 45 minutes or until the cake tests done. Cool in the pan for 5 minutes. Pour the Rum Sauce over the cake. Cool in the pan for 15 minutes longer. Remove to a wire rack to cool completely; do not remove the 9×13-inch cake from the pan.

Yield: 12 to 15 servings

RUM SAUCE

¹/₂ cup (1 stick) butter
1 cup sugar
¹/₄ cup rum
¹/₄ cup water

Combine the butter, sugar, rum and water in a saucepan. Bring to a boil, stirring constantly. Cool before spreading over the cake.

Pumpkin Lemon Cake

1 (3-ounce) package lemon instant
   pudding mix
3/4 cup (1 1/2 sticks) butter, softened
1 3/4 cups sugar
2 eggs
1 cup pumpkin
1 cup milk
1 teaspoon vanilla extract
2 1/4 cups flour
1 teaspoon baking powder
1 teaspoon baking soda
1 teaspoon salt
1 teaspoon cinnamon
1 teaspoon ginger
1/4 teaspoon allspice
1/4 teaspoon ground cloves

Prepare the pudding mix using the package directions. Chill for at least 8 to 10 hours. Cream the butter and sugar in a mixing bowl until light and fluffy. Add the eggs and pumpkin and mix well. Stir in the milk and vanilla. Combine the flour, baking powder, baking soda, salt, cinnamon, ginger, allspice and cloves. Add to the creamed mixture gradually, mixing well after each addition. Reserve 1 1/2 cups of the batter. Pour the remaining batter into a greased and floured bundt pan. Spread the lemon pudding over the center of the batter, away from the sides of the pan. Layer the remaining batter over the top. Bake at 350 degrees for 1 hour or until the cake tests done. Cool in the pan for 1 hour. Invert onto a serving plate. Serve with whipped cream if desired.

Yield: 10 servings

Grandma Walters' Pumpkin Cake

1 (2-layer) package yellow cake mix
$1/2$ cup (1 stick) butter, melted
4 eggs
1 (29-ounce) can solid-pack
  pumpkin
$1/2$ cup packed brown sugar
$1^{1}/_{2}$ (12-ounce) cans evaporated
  milk
2 tablespoons pumpkin pie spice
$1/2$ teaspoon cinnamon
$1/2$ teaspoon nutmeg
$1/4$ cup sugar
$1^{1}/_{2}$ teaspoons cinnamon
$1/4$ cup ($1/2$ stick) butter, cut into
  chunks

*R*eserve 1 cup of the cake mix for the topping. Combine the remaining cake mix, $1/2$ cup butter and 1 egg in a mixing bowl and blend well. Spread in a greased 9×13-inch cake dish, pressing firmly into an even layer. Combine 3 eggs, the pumpkin, brown sugar, evaporated milk, pumpkin pie spice, $1/2$ teaspoon cinnamon and the nutmeg in a mixing bowl and blend well. Spread over the cake layer. Combine the reserved 1 cup cake mix, sugar, $1^{1}/_{2}$ teaspoons cinnamon and $1/4$ cup butter in a bowl and mix until crumbly. Sprinkle over the pumpkin mixture. Bake at 350 degrees for 50 to 60 minutes or until golden brown. Serve warm or cold.

Yield: 10 to 15 servings

Pumpkin Chocolate Chip Muffins

1 (15-ounce) can solid-pack pumpkin
4 eggs, beaten
2 cups sugar
1½ cups vegetable oil
3 cups flour
2 teaspoons baking powder
2 teaspoons baking soda
1 teaspoon cinnamon
1 teaspoon salt
12 ounces semisweet chocolate chips

Combine the pumpkin, eggs, sugar, and oil in a bowl and blend well. Combine the flour, baking powder, baking soda, cinnamon and salt in a bowl. Add to the pumpkin mixture and stir just until mixed. Fold in the chocolate chips. Spoon into 24 greased or paper-lined muffin cups. Bake at 400 degrees for 15 to 20 minutes or until a wooden pick inserted in the center comes out clean. Remove from the pan and cool on a wire rack.

Yield: 24 muffins

Great Pumpkin Cookies

2 cups flour
1 1/3 cups quick-cooking oats
1 teaspoon baking soda
1 teaspoon cinnamon
1/2 teaspoon salt
1 cup (2 sticks) butter
1 cup solid-pack pumpkin
1 cup packed brown sugar
1 cup sugar
1 egg
1 teaspoon vanilla extract
3/4 cup chopped walnuts
3/4 cup raisins

Combine the flour, oats, baking soda, cinnamon and salt in a bowl. Beat the butter in a mixing bowl until light and fluffy. Add the pumpkin, brown sugar, sugar, egg, and vanilla and mix well. Stir in the flour mixture. Add the walnuts and raisins. Drop by 1/4 cupfuls and spread into 3-inch circles on a nonstick cookie sheet. Bake at 350 degrees for 14 to 16 minutes or until firm and light brown. Cool on a wire rack. Decorate as desired with icing, chocolate chips, candies, raisins or nuts.

Yield: 20 cookies

Note: These cookies should be soft, not hard and crunchy.

Chinese New Year Cookies

12 ounces butterscotch chips
1 (3-ounce) can Chinese noodles
1 can peanuts

Melt the butterscotch chips in a double boiler over hot water, stirring occasionally. Remove from the heat. Stir in the Chinese noodles and peanuts. Drop by teaspoonfuls onto waxed paper. Chill until firm.

Yield: 3 dozen cookies

Rum Balls

3 cups crushed vanilla wafers
1 cup confectioners' sugar
1/2 cup whiskey or rum
1 1/2 teaspoons baking cocoa
1 cup walnuts, chopped
Confectioners' sugar

Combine the vanilla wafers, confectioners' sugar, whiskey, baking cocoa and walnuts in a bowl and mix well. Shape into small balls. Roll in confectioners' sugar.

Yield: about 4 dozen servings

Note: There is no baking required for these little treats.

Mom's Peanut Butter Fudge

1 cup (2 sticks) margarine
1 cup peanut butter
1 teaspoon vanilla extract
1 (1-pound) package confectioners'
* sugar*

Heat the margarine and peanut butter in a saucepan over low heat, stirring until smooth. Stir in the vanilla and confectioners' sugar. Remove from the heat and mix well. Press into a buttered 9×9-inch baking dish. Chill until firm. Cut into squares.

Yield: 30 to 40 servings

Stained Glass Window Candy

12 ounces milk chocolate chips
2 tablespoons butter
1 egg, beaten
3¹/2 cups colored marshmallows
1 package coconut

Melt the chocolate chips and butter in a saucepan over low heat, stirring until smooth. Remove from the heat. Beat in the egg. Let stand until slightly cool. Stir in the marshmallows. Sprinkle the coconut over a large sheet of waxed paper. Spoon the marshmallow mixture in a rectangular shape over the coconut. Shape into a log using the waxed paper. Chill for at least 5 hours. Cut into ¹/4-inch slices.

Yield: 12 or more servings

Mints

2¹/2 cups confectioners' sugar
3 ounces cream cheese, softened
¹/2 teaspoon peppermint extract
¹/3 cup sugar

Combine the confectioners' sugar, cream cheese and peppermint extract in a bowl and mix well. Knead until a dough forms. Roll into small balls. Coat with the sugar. Press into candy molds. Remove from molds and serve.

Yield: 10 or more servings

Contributors

Jane Altmeyer	Debbie Gordon	Meredith McKinley
Margaret Ball	Stephanie Grove	Zoe Metcalf
Sarah Barickman	Laura Haden	Tammy Miller
Wendy Barbeau	Rhonda Hager	Shirley Milton
Alecia Blair	Rhonda Haley	Nikki Mullinix
Karen Blair	Janet Hart	Dawn Nazzaro
Stephanie Bloch	Karen Hartley	Jennifer Nettles
Anne Bopp	Heather Hartong	Denise Peterson
Cristen Breski	Deane Hawkins	Lea Ridenhour
Terri Buck	Sherry Hennen	Karen Rine
Saun Capehart	Wendy Hinerman	Alison Robinson
Nancy Jo Clarke	Deanna Hoffmann	Amy Shafer
Jodi Cook	Angi Howell-Tennant	Shawna Shepherd
Danielle Cross McCracken	Becket Ihlenfeld	Lisa Sims
Betsy Delk	Kathy Irvin	Libby Slater
Karen Diorio	Charl Kappel	Amy Smith
Kelly Dobkin	Shelly Klatt	Maria Smith
Linda Elliott	Jane Krupica	Erikka Storch
Margaret Ewing	Christine Kuhn	Sheila Tarr-Stiglich
Ginny Favede	Jennifer Magruder	Shawn Turak
Ruth Foose	Ruth Mann	Ann Viewig
Rosemary M. Front	Linda Mason	Diana Walter
Danielle Futey	Jennifer Mason	Debbie Wilkinson
Rene George	Kathleen McDermott	Betty Worls
Donna Glass		Marlene Yahn

Other Friends

Donald Barickman	Sandra Melchiorre
Bill Blair	Dorcas Mitchell
Marlo Campbell	Susie Orr
Molly Cipley	Brad Paisley
Thelma Cook	Dave Trunnell
Goldie Lanos	

Financial Friends

Artworks Around Town Gallery and Art Center	PPG Industries, Inc.
Carol Bisset	Mary (Weaver) Renner
Stephanie H. Bloch	Bob Robinson Chevrolet-Oldsmobile-Cadillac, Inc.
Mary Eleanor Colvin	Shawn Turak
Direct Maytag Home Appliance	Beth Weaver
Ruth B. Mann	Eleanor Weaver
Shirley T. Milton	Shirley Weaver
June Paull	Debbie Wright

Substitutions

RECIPE CALLS FOR	YOU MAY SUBSTITUTE
1 square unsweetened chocolate	3 tablespoons unsweetened cocoa powder plus 1 tablespoon butter/margarine
1 cup cake flour	1 cup less 2 tablespoons all-purpose flour
2 tablespoons flour (for thickening)	1 tablespoon cornstarch
1 teaspoon baking powder	$1/4$ teaspoon baking soda plus $1/2$ teaspoon cream of tartar plus $1/4$ teaspoon cornstarch
1 cup corn syrup	1 cup sugar plus $1/4$ cup additional liquid used in recipe
1 cup milk	$1/2$ cup evaporated milk plus $1/2$ cup water
1 cup buttermilk or sour milk	1 tablespoon vinegar or lemon juice plus enough milk to make 1 cup
1 cup sour cream (for baking)	1 cup plain yogurt
1 cup firmly packed brown sugar	1 cup sugar plus 2 tablespoons molasses
1 teaspoon lemon juice	$1/4$ teaspoon vinegar (not balsamic)
$1/4$ cup chopped onion	1 tablespoon instant minced
1 clove garlic	$1/8$ teaspoon garlic powder
2 cups tomato sauce	$3/4$ cup tomato paste plus 1 cup water
1 tablespoon prepared mustard	1 teaspoon dry mustard plus 1 tablespoon water

Spice Substitutions

INSTEAD OF	USE
Apple pie spice, 1 teaspoon	$1/2$ teaspoon ground cinnamon, $1/4$ teaspoon ground nutmeg, $1/8$ teaspoon ground allspice, and a dash ground cloves or ginger
Ground allspice	Ground cinnamon, nutmeg, or cloves
Ground anise	Crushed fennel seeds or a few drops anise extract
Ground cardamom	Ground ginger
Chili powder	Dash of hot bottled pepper sauce, plus equal measures ground oregano and cumin
Ground cinnamon	Ground nutmeg or allspice (use only a quarter of the amount called for in the recipe)
Ground cloves	Ground allspice, cinnamon, or nutmeg
Ground cumin	Chili powder
Garlic, 1 clove	$1/8$ teaspoon garlic powder
Ground ginger	Ground allspice, cinnamon, mace, or nutmeg
Ground mace	Ground allspice, cinnamon, ginger, or nutmeg
Powdered mustard, 1 teaspoon	1 tablespoon prepared mustard
Ground nutmeg	Ground cinnamon, ginger, or mace
Pumpkin pie spice, 1 teaspoon	$1/2$ teaspoon ground cinnamon, $1/4$ teaspoon ground ginger, $1/4$ teaspoon ground allspice, and $1/8$ teaspoon ground nutmeg
Ground red pepper	Hot pepper sauce
Dash ground saffron	$1/4$ teaspoon ground turmeric

Equivalents

MEASURE	EQUALS
Teaspoons	
Under $1/8$ teaspoon	Dash or pinch
$1^1/2$ teaspoons	$1/2$ tablespoon
3 teaspoons	1 tablespoon
Tablespoons	
1 tablespoon	3 teaspoons
4 tablespoons	$1/4$ cup
$5^1/3$ tablespoons	$1/3$ cup
8 tablespoons	$1/2$ cup
$10^2/3$ tablespoons	$2/3$ cup
16 tablespoons	1 cup
Cups	
$1/4$ cup	4 tablespoons
$1/3$ cup	$5^1/3$ tablespoons
$1/2$ cup	8 tablespoons
$1/2$ cup	$1/4$ pint
$2/3$ cup	$10^2/3$ tablespoons
1 cup	16 tablespoons
1 cup	$1/2$ pint
2 cups	1 pint
4 cups	1 quart
Liquid Measures	
2 tablespoons	1 fluid ounce
3 tablespoons	1 jigger
$1/4$ cup	2 fluid ounces
$1/2$ cup	4 fluid ounces
1 cup	8 fluid ounces

Measure for Measure

AMOUNT	MEASURE	AMOUNT	MEASURE
Berries		**Dried Beans and Peas**	
1 pint	2^1/$_4$ cups	1 cup	2^1/$_4$ cups cooked
Butter or Margarine		**Herbs**	
^{1}/$_2$ stick	^{1}/$_4$ cup or 4 tablespoons	1 tablespoon fresh	1 teaspoon dried
1 pound	4 sticks or 2 cups	**Pasta**	
Cheese		8 ounces elbow macaroni	4 cups cooked
8 ounces cream cheese	1 cup	8 ounces medium-wide noodles	3^3/$_4$ cups cooked
8 ounces cottage cheese	1 cup	8 ounces fine noodles	5^1/$_2$ cups cooked
4 ounces Parmesan, grated	1^1/$_4$ cups	8 ounces spaghetti	4 cups cooked
Chocolate		**Rice**	
1 square	1 ounce	1 cup white	3 cups cooked
1 (6-ounce) package semisweet pieces	1 cup	1 cup converted	4 cups cooked
		1 cup instant	1^1/$_2$ cups cooked
Cookies		1 cup brown	3 to 4 cups cooked
For 1 cup of crumbs:			
19 chocolate wafers		**Sugar**	
22 vanilla wafers		1 pound granulated	2 cups
14 graham cracker squares		1 pound brown, firmly packed	2^1/$_4$ cups
Cream		1 pound confectioners'	4^1/$_2$ cups
1 cup heavy cream	2 cups whipped		

Index

Index

Index

Index

Wild! Wonderful!

A Cookbook With Flair

The Junior League of Wheeling, Inc.
907 1/2 National Road
Wheeling, West Virginia 26003
304-232-3164

YOUR ORDER	QUANTITY	TOTAL
Wild! Wonderful! at $18.95 per book		$
West Virginia residents add 6.0% sales tax		$
Postage and handling at $3.50 per book		$
	Total	$

Name _____

Street Address _____

City _____ State _____ Zip _____

Telephone _____

Method of Payment: [   ] MasterCard   [   ] VISA
[   ] Check payable to Junior League of Wheeling, Inc.

Account Number _____ Expiration Date _____

Signature _____

Photocopies will be accepted.

191